Pathway to an Addiction Free Lifestyle

Pathway to an Addiction Free Lifestyle

By Rory C. Folsom & Steven D. Duby

Published by
MIDNIGHT EXPRESS BOOKS

Pathway to an *Addiction Free* Lifestyle

2012 Rory C. Folsom & Steven D. Duby

All Rights Reserved, Breaking Free grants no assignable permission to reproduce for resale or redistribution. This License is limited to the individual purchaser and does not extend to others. Permission to reproduce these materials for any other purpose must be obtained in writing from publisher.

ISBN-10: 0988806363

ISBN-13: 978-0-9888063-6-8

DISCLAIMER:

This book and information herein is for educational and inspirational purpose only and not to be used for self-treatment. Likewise, information contained herein is not intended or implied to be a substitute for professional medical advice or a replacement for any treatment. Always seek the advice of your physician or other qualified health provider for all medical problems, treatments, or with any questions you may have regarding a medical condition.

Published by
MIDNIGHT EXPRESS BOOKS
POBox 69
Berryville AR 72616
(870) 210-3772
MEBooks1@yahoo.com

Pathway to an Addiction Free Lifestyle

By Rory C. Folsom & Steven D. Duby

Dedication

Breaking Free is dedicated to the first participants in Ironwood State Prison, who assisted in the beta test for the program

Acknowledgements

Thank you to all of the Addiction Treatment Specialists, Mr. J. Kizler, Mr. M. Hauser, Mr. M. Leslie, Mr. J. Bradford and Mr. D. Mitchell for their varied and individually invaluable input in bringing this program into being.

A special thanks to:

Mr. R. McClain, (Addiction Treatment Specialist), for all of his tireless work and dedication in helping develop and proof the materials used for the program. Also, Mr. J. White Jr. for obtaining the proper audience to help make the program possible and for its success.

A Very Special thanks to:

Mathew Cates, former Under Secretary, California Department of Corrections and Rehabilitation,
Dave Long, Warden, Ironwood State Prison
Patrick Covello, Captain, Ironwood State Prison – for your visions into making a difference in many lives.
Also, to the GOGI family, and for all of your inspiration; thank you.

About the Authors

Rory C. Folsom, American Indian former combat United States Marine, was incarcerated for a drug related homicide. Rory became involved with youth diversion and drug treatment groups since 1985. For the past twenty seven years he has became a Drug and Alcohol Treatment Specialist. He also has extensive list of other academic achievements and college degrees. During this time he also has become a Certified Relaxation Therapist, Ordained Minister/Spiritual Healer and Diplomat of Earth Stewarts with the International Assembly of Spiritual Healers and Earth Stewarts. With all his diverse knowledge concerning one on one, group and 12-step treatment process, he has developed the Breaking Free program. This combines the best of all of the different areas for a clear road for long term recovery.

Steven D. Duby served in the United States Air Force. He has spent over twenty-five years incarcerated in the State of California for a second degree murder. While incarcerated, he obtained two college degrees (Business Management and General Studies). He became an Addictions Treatment Specialist and has certification(s) as a Braille-Transcriber. Steven has been working with at-risk-teens since 1993 which is part of his passion to help the community. After decades of AA/NA programs, experiencing extensive diversity within the Drug/Alcohol Counseling Community, Steven had the distinct privilege to co-author the "Breaking Free" treatment program.

Pathway to an *Addictive Free* Lifestyle

TABLE OF CONTENTS

Program Introduction i

Weekly Plans iii

Week 1 Lesson Plan 1

Week 2 Lesson Plan 15

Week 3 Lesson Plan 33

Week 4 Lesson Plan 53

Week 5 Lesson Plan 83

Week 6 Lesson Plan 111

Week 7 Lesson Plan 141

Week 8 Lesson Plan 157

Appendix 'A' Participation & Confidential Agreement A-1

Appendix 'B' Initial Assessment B-1

Appendix 'C' List of Current Videos & CDs C-1

Appendix 'D' List of Pamphlets D-1

Appendix 'E' Exit Plan for Post Release E-1

Appendix 'F' Mind Mapping F-1

Appendix 'G' Life Plan & Relapse Prevention Plan G-1

Handouts H-1

Rory C. Folsom & Steven D. Duby

Program Introduction

Breaking Free is an intensive eight (8) week substance abuse and behavioral self-awareness treatment program that contains several key components. This will be an in-patient / out-patient program and there will be a one-on-one counseling component as needed. The foundation is based upon the concept of sobriety along with mental, physical and social wellness. *Breaking Free* also instills the *EACH ONE TEACH ONE* principles. The program is designed with three (3) weekly group sessions as well as three (3) self-development homework assignments to be completed during the week. This allows Phase One of the program to be completed within the eight (8) weeks.

Recovery and Social Wellness draws on several different philosophies and practices of substance abuse group therapy, one-on-one and the 12-step process. Along with these practices 'Breaking Free' will integrate self-awareness, anger management, and Bio-Psycho-Social aspects of living within our society norms both in and out of institutional settings.

Recovery and Social Wellness equates into a well-balanced human being. A balanced person is one with a developed sense of responsibility, insight, and remorse. This person can be strongly connected to the principals, laws, and values of the world they live in. The *EACH ONE TEACH ONE* principal states that everyone has value, and everyone has at-least one something (knowledge, life experiences, etc.), that can help someone else.

Treatment Curriculum Outline

As each individual enters *Breaking Free*, they will sign an Agreement of Participation. Then the individual will be given a complete Initial Assessment and a Participant Confidential Statement Agreement Form.

The schedule will be designed for full group participation, three (3) days a week in a common area, and will consist of a Self-Development Assignment after each session. All assignments will need to be completed as instructed or the individual will be re-accessed for program review.

One must take responsibility for one's own *Recovery and Social Wellness*. Integrity is a key component to the success of *Breaking Free* and the recovery process. *Breaking Free* is also developed and designed to utilize Substance Abuse Treatment Specialists. If a participant misses one (1) group session or assignment, without prior authorization, the participant's program status will be re-accessed, and the participant will not be allowed to graduate or receive any credit for attending any previous sessions. The treatment course will last eight (8) weeks. Once each individual graduates it does not mean it is the end of the self-awareness program and their commitment to *Recovery and Social Wellness*. A Substance Abuse Treatment Specialist counselor can be assigned for one-on-one follow-up / Relapse Prevention Program.

Along with the Substance Abuse Treatment Specialist counselors this program will have the ability to address the issues and the consequences of a person's decision making, such as intravenous drug usage and tattooing. Counselors will provide the participant's current medical health information concerning HIV/AIDS, Hepatitis, Staph / MRSA, etc., and other issues that affects their substance abuse. The exchange of information about infectious diseases and high-risk behavior can have a major impact on public health and public safety. This self-awareness and behavior treatment program will have the ability to empower a kind of cultural change that will benefit participants, their families, and society in general.

The ultimate responsibility of changing culture lies within its members. The most effective means to change the culture, or change some of the socially accepted norms within any setting, is to get the training to participants through the self-awareness, to model and assist in facilitating a positive behavior change in general. We must change the stinking thinking of the individuals by providing a Drug / Alcohol, Behavioral, and Self-Awareness Program which promotes wellness of the mind, body, and spirit of every person. This will help each person to obtain their human potential for a positive, law-abiding life style.

We must understand that substance abuse stems from deeper and wider problems in each individual. *Breaking Free* has the ability to allow the participants to look into themselves not only in a group setting but also within a one-on-one setting. This is why the program has options for each individual to explore based on their needs. With the individual addressing the problems that have caused them to continue to use (abuse) drugs and/or alcohol, they can now change their thought process which allows a strong foundation for long-term recovery.

While most people are visual learners, learning also occurs through auditory and tactile means. The treatment program's personal development information therefore uses a variety of teaching methods. Some are: lectures; discussions (both group and one-on-one); guest speakers; educational audio/video tapes; pamphlets; written materials; lesson plans; worksheets; posters and role-plays.

This program design deals with not only the direct aspects of substance abuse but empowers each individual to have the insight into personal problems which lead to the reasons for prolonged substance abuse. With this knowledge they can construct a realistic relapse prevention plan.

Pathway to an *Addiction Free* Lifestyle

WEEK ONE LESSON PLAN

SESSION 1:

Complete an Introduction. Each individual will be given the Participation and Confidential Agreement as well as the Initial Assessment documents. Each form will be carefully reviewed by the participant. After the participant agrees to the terms of participation they will sign the voluntary agreement (Participation and Confidential Agreement). Then the counselors will help the group to complete the Initial Assessment documents. A file folder will be given to each participant to keep a complete record of program assignments and other related information documents.

ASSIGNMENT:

Individuals will have to complete the Personal Development Assignment on 'Responsibility.'

SESSION 2:

What is Dependence? Principles of Addiction: When, Where, Why, How, and What has made the individual make the choice to use the first altering substance. What is the 'Principals of the Need' to use more? Upon learning these principles we then introduce how to integrate a 12-Step process that can be used in making better decisions. The building of life skills allows the participant to become aware of how our emotional behavior leads to the use and abuse of the substance of our choice. Then the introduction of an Action and Re-Action Results Personal Development Assignment, on how our individual actions took place and how we re-acted which leads to the results of being substance abuse and finely being in this group today.

ASSIGNMENT:

Complete the Personal Development Assignment: how our actions and re-actions resulted in our life path of destruction.

SESSION 3:

Complete an overview of the week's work and also gain an understanding of how the immune system gets damaged through substance abuse and other irresponsible actions. These actions by the substance abuser can lead to permanent and / or long-lasting health problems.

ASSISNMENT:

Complete the Personal Development Assignment: Immune System

Rory C. Folsom & Steven D. Duby

Pathway to an *Addictive Free* Lifestyle

WEEK TWO LESSON PLAN

SESSION 1:

Insight into Life Development, the group will be presented with what is insight, and knowing how to understand life development in regards to 'Recovery and Social Wellness.' Living life on life's terms. Understanding the difference between living a 'fear based' or a 'love based' lifestyle, and how it can contribute to substance abuse. Then review the Personal Development Assignment, concerning what triggers the emotional stimulus life style awareness.

ASSIGNMENT:

Complete the Personal Development Assignment: 'fear based' or 'love based' life style and what emotional stimuli cause and affect substance abuse.

SESSION 2:

Victimization: Your Victim(s), Self, Family, Community. The group will be introduced into what is Victimization. Who is really affected by the world of substance abuse? What are the aspects to oneself, family and community at large? The group is given guidance into how to stop the cycle of victimization and introduce this concept into their Life Plan.

ASSIGNMENT:

Complete the Personal Development Assignment: Introduction into the Life Plan.

SESSION 3:

The 12-Step verses Group Therapy. Integration of the 12-Step process into the Life Plan with the understanding of the five (5) stages of recovery. Each stage will be discussed. Then the group will be given the Personal Development Assignment with regards to their individual stage at this time of their recovery.

ASSIGNMENT:

Complete the Personal Development Assignment: Stages of recovery, the 12-Step process and Life Planning.

Pathway to an *Addiction Free* Lifestyle
WEEK THREE LESSON PLAN

SESSION 1:

The group presentation will cover what are and how to live by principals, laws and values. They will be given compare and contrasting ideas of each subject while having an open discussion on why we must live by these concepts since their best thinking while under substances had their lives out of control. Then cover what leads to substance abuse and all the associated problems with their substance abuse. Why it is important to have good principals, living by rules of society (laws) and not just thinking of one self. Explain the need to put value on all life. Then an explanation of the results of failing to live by these concepts, along with one of the by-products which is anger. So they will be given an understanding of what it is and what is not.

ASSIGNMENT:

Complete the Personal Development Assignment: anger and how it affects them, which leads to most substance abuse.

SESSION 2:

The group session will consist of how to identify self-talk within our perception. How do we treat the perception of negative self-talk why our perception may or may not be what is the truth. How do we change our actions to fit the perception of right or wrong, so we do not fall back into substance abuse. Then cover the Personal Development Assignment on the Reality Model and how it relates to our perceptions.

ASSIGNMENT:

Complete the Personal Development Assignment: The Reality Model.

SESSION 3:

The group discussion will direct its attention to how we identify ourselves and how we think the world around us perceives us. We discuss how culture identity has the different affects of substance abuse on individuals. Then the Personal Development Assignment concerning how they believe or perceive how their culture influenced their substance abuse life style.

ASSISNMENT:

Complete the Personal Development Assignment: Culture beliefs and substance abuse.

Pathway to an *Addiction Free* Lifestyle
WEEK FOUR LESSON PLAN

SESSION 1:

The group presentation will move into understanding what path they have taken in their life with substance abuse, how much destruction has been done and how to correct any further destruction. Learn how to identify themselves and / or how society may perceive them. Then the need to the making of amends to those they have harmed. They will also be introduced to how each of the drugs (substances) affects the mind, body, and spirit. Then they will be given a Personal Development Assignment dealing with the different drugs/alcohol and chemicals which have had a direct and long lasting affect within the human body.

ASSIGNMENT:

Complete the Personal Development Assignment: Human Body and Affects of Substance Abuse.

SESSION 2:

The group will be given the opportunity to understand and learn how to express in a clear, open communication style their self-awareness. Teach the need for one to be able to express what you need or no one else will be able to help you. Then the individuals will be given another overview of the Reality Model.

ASSIGNMENT:

Complete the Personal Development Assignment: The Reality Model.

SESSION 3:

During this group the discussion will be concerning the differences between 'Over-the-Counter' substances and 'Street' substances. This group will discuss the affects of alcohol verses chemicals and how their affects are different over a short- and long-term period(s) of use.

ASSIGNMENT:

Complete the Personal Development Assignment: Different Alcohol and Drug Affects on their health.

Rory C. Folsom & Steven D. Duby

Pathway to an *Addiction Free* Lifestyle

WEEK FIVE LESSON PLAN

SESSION 1:

This group will discuss co-dependence and what the 12-Step process can be if brought into a life style of 'Recovery and Social Wellness'. Each individual will be given information on how to identify and deal with co-dependency issues that can arise through treatment programs. This will give each individual the power to live life on life terms, knowing their strengths and weaknesses. At the end of the group they will be able to start to apply the Reality Model to their own daily lives, also with short and long-term life plan goals. The Personal Development Assignment will be discussed concerning individuals time management.

ASSIGNMENT:

Complete the Personal Development Assignment: Time Management (How to manage time will keep the individuals from relapse ideology)

SESSION 2:

This group will be given information and guidance on how self-motivation life skills and goal setting will help them from relapsing to the substance abuse life style. The lack of motivation is one of the biggest down falls for an addict. If you can motivate someone to make very short term goals, like completing the assignments or just to do one thing every day then move on to two days, etc., from this you are able to build an individual's confidence to break their addiction. Next thing you know their emotional health starts to get stronger. Then more motivation sets in. Then long-term goal and 'Recovery and Social Wellness' life style comes into being and this all is part of a positive cycle rather than the destructive substance abuse cycle. Lastly, the Personal Development Assignment will be discussed concerning the treatments for the different viruses that are contracted via substance abuse such as HIV/AIDS, Hepatitis A, B & C, etc.

ASSIGNMENT:

Self-motivation questions.

SESSION 3:

This group session will deal directly with what is Insight & Remorse. The reason why the individuals need to know what Insight is, is to allow them to truly understand their addiction in every aspect and how to take ownership of their individual recovery. Remorse, how can or what would anyone want to change regarding their past actions. Also, if they can not understand or comprehend the hurt and pain they have caused directly or indirectly during their path of substance abuse, this needs to be dealt with as part of their Insight.

ASSIGNMENT:

Complete the Personal Development Assignment: Insight & Remorse.

_____

_____

_____

_____

_____

_____

_____

_____

_____

_____

_____

_____

_____

_____

_____

_____

_____

Pathway to an *Addictive Free* Lifestyle

WEEK SIX LESSON PLAN

SESSION 1:

During this group discussion we will identify and introduce the individuals to what is stress and how to deal with it without turning to substances abuse. Methods of stress reduction such as: Creative Visualization, meditation, etc., are introduced to the group. The Personal Development Assignment will be discussed regarding coping skills, stress reactivity, and then taking control of one's own stress management.

ASSIGNMENT:

Complete the Personal Development Assignment: Stress related issues dealing with day-to-day issues and what to put into the individuals Life Plan for relapse prevention.

SESSION 2:

This group discussion is dealing with the Type 'A' behavior pattern and how to understand it and overcome the need to be in control over all aspects of one's life when in fact there are many issues we have no control. This discussion will involve the understanding and the importance of Forgiveness and Spiritual Health dimensions of recovery. The Personal Development Assignment will be discussed concerning Forgiveness and Behavior Patterns.

ASSIGNMENT:

Complete the Personal Development Assignment: the different Forgiveness and Behavior Patterns.

SESSION 3:

This group session will deal with the different aspects of traumatic events in each individual's life which may have caused a condition of Post-Traumatic Stress Disorder (PTSD). PTSD causes many emotional effects that the individual may not know why they are acting the way they are and until you do the personal inventory, this individual will be at a loss. Then discussion of the individual's family of origin and their role in the family is, and what it is suppose to be. Then there will be an open discussion as what we are: as a benefit or the creator of pain and loss.

ASSIGNMENT:

Complete the Personal Development Assignment: The Family Role and how traumatic events in one's life could cause emotional distress that could lead back to substance abuse life style.

Rory C. Folsom & Steven D. Duby

Pathway to an *Addictive Free* Lifestyle

WEEK SEVEN LESSON PLAN

SESSION 1:

This group will cover the understanding and developing of what is called 'Mind Mapping.' This will direct the individuals on the polarity of life with and without substance abuse. This session will be completed by asking the individuals to answer how they think their life would look without illegal substances, or if they continue to use illegal substance what their life will look like. This will guide them to thinking about social factors and life cycles. The Personal Development Assignment will direct them to complete several 'Mind Mapping' questions.

ASSIGNMENT:

Complete the Personal Development Assignment: 'Mind Mapping.'

SESSION 2:

This group will discuss how Gender Roles and Gender Ideology can contribute to self-awareness. How does it play in substance abuse and anger issues that will cause relapse problems dealing with our place in normal society? Also, how peer pressures add to the problems. How these issues can lead to risky behavior.

ASSIGNMENT:

Complete the Personal Development Assignment: conditions of Risky Behavior (i.e., drinking, drug usage, etc.)

SESSION 3:

This group session will cover Family Dynamics in the different areas of substance abuse. There will also be a review on the family history and substance abuse leading to a continuous cycle of substance abuse within the family unit. It will cover both inside and outside of an institutional setting.

ASSIGNMENT:

Complete the Personal Development Assignment: family dynamics and how to improve and stop the family cycle of substance abuse.

Pathway to an *Addiction Free* Lifestyle

WEEK EIGHT LESSON PLAN

SESSION 1:

This group discussion will cover several areas of survival roles and coping mechanisms. These areas include how to bring the self-awareness, anger management learned skills, and 'Recovery and Social Wellness' techniques into the day-to-day life skills. These ideas and practices can be implemented into the Life Plan. The Personal Development Assignment will be completing the Life Plan.

ASSIGNMENT:

Complete the Personal Development Assignment: completing the program Life Plan Outline.

SESSION 2:

The group will be given a comprehensive relapse prevention plan outline. How and where to find and obtain a sponsor. The different programs and support systems that needs to be in place. These important issues need to be clear, concise, and honestly brought into the open for a clear understanding of them. Then we will do a complete program overview and the individuals requesting one-on-one counseling will be assigned to a substance abuse specialist for continued relapse prevention and social needs.

ASSIGNMENT:

Complete the Personal Development Assignment: the ending individual program.

... Graduation Day!

Rory C. Folsom & Steven D. Duby

Pathway to an *Addictive Free* Lifestyle

WEEK ONE

Learning Objectives

- ❖ Introduction / Understanding Responsibility
- ❖ Self Development Assignment
- ❖ What is Dependence?
- ❖ Action & Re-Action Results
- ❖ 12-Step Process / Life Skills
- ❖ Immune System Issues, Hepatitis

Pathway to an *Addictive Free* Lifestyle

GROUP DISCUSSION

WEEK ONE

SESSION I

INTRODUCTION

Complete an Introduction. Each individual will be given the Participation and Confidential Agreement Form as well as the Initial Assessment document. Each form will be carefully reviewed by the participant. After the participant agrees to the terms of participation they will sign the voluntary agreement (Participation and Confidential Agreement Form). Then the counselors will help the group to complete the Initial Assessment documents. A file folder will be given to each participant to keep a complete record of program assignments and other related informational documents.

_____

_____

_____

_____

_____

_____

_____

_____

_____

_____

_____

_____

_____

_____

Pathway to an *Addictive Free* Lifestyle

PERSONAL DEVELOPMENT ASSIGNMENT

WEEK ONE

RESPONSIBILITY

This assignment is one where we must look up the word 'Responsibility' and write it out:

RESPONSIBILTY:

_____
_____
_____
_____
_____

Write a statement about the conscious choice to actively seek out and identify those character flaws inside of yourself that made / make it okay for you to commit criminal acts and hurt yourself and others by using drugs / alcohol or destructive behavior.

_____
_____
_____
_____
_____
_____
_____
_____
_____

Rory C. Folsom & Steven D. Duby

Pathway to an *Addictive Free* Lifestyle

GROUP DISCUSSION

WEEK ONE

SESSION 2

WHAT IS DEPENDENCE

Drug dependence is a general term indicating that a person's substance abuse has led to the user's experiencing uncontrollable and unpleasant mood state that in turn leads the user to use the substance in doses or ways that result in adverse consequences. (Newcomb & Bentler, 1989)

Terms that are synonymous with drug dependence are **substance dependence and substance abuse**. The former term is used in The Diagnostic and Statistical Manual of Mental Disorders-IV (DSM-IV), in which a diagnosis is made on the basis of several specific criteria. These criteria are very similar to those for drug addiction, which was defined over 35 years ago by the World Health Organization (WHO) as a state of periodic or chronic intoxication detrimental to the individual or society.

We must understand the reasons of the **Psychological Dependence** which is referred to as a strong compulsion or desire to experience the effects of a drug because it produces pleasure or reduces psychological discomfort. (Chap. 6, Drug & Human Behavior pg. 115)

Group Exercise:

List at least three things (items) you are psychologically dependant on.

1. _____
2. _____
3. _____

Do you feel that you can function each day without using these things (items)? Please state why or why not.

_____
_____
_____
_____

Pathway to an *Addictive Free* Lifestyle

PERSONAL DEVELOPMENT ASSIGNMENT

WEEK ONE

ACTIONS AND RE-ACTION RESULTS

Write a short essay concerning your actions during the times you were under the influence as well as your behavior. How others reacted to you and one person you may have hurt during that time.

_____
_____
_____
_____
_____
_____
_____
_____
_____
_____
_____
_____
_____
_____
_____
_____
_____

Rory C. Folsom & Steven D. Duby

Pathway to an *Addiction Free* Lifestyle
GROUP DISCUSSION

WEEK ONE

SESSION 3

12 STEP PROCESS / LIFE SKILLS AND
AN OVERVIEW OF THE 1st WEEK'S WORK

The group discussion will be an overview of the first week's work. It also includes an understanding of how our immune system gets damaged through the substance abuse and other irresponsible actions that take place during substance abuse. We will have an open discussion on the 12 step process / life skills and the participants will have a take home assignment to complete by the next group session.

_____

_____

_____

_____

_____

_____

_____

_____

_____

_____

_____

_____

_____

_____

_____

Pathway to an *Addictive Free* Lifestyle

PERSONAL DEVELOPMENT ASSIGNMENT

WEEK ONE

IMMUNE SYSTEMS

Complete the Personal Development Assignment on the Immune System and answer the questions from the Immune System handout on page H-3.

WEEK TWO

Learning Objective

- ❖ Insight into Life Development
- ❖ Fear Based and Loved Based Life Styles
- ❖ Analyzing Victimization: Victims, Self, Family and Community
- ❖ Introduction to the Life Plan
- ❖ 12-Steps versus Group Therapy
- ❖ Five stages of Recovery

Pathway to an *Addictive Free* Lifestyle

GROUP DISCUSSION

WEEK TWO

SESSION 1

INSIGHT INTO LIFE DEVELOPMENT

INSIGHT: Insight has three (3) major parts that relates to substance abuse/behavior.

WEBSTER'S New College Dictionary: 1. the ability to see and understand clearly the inner nature of things, esp. by intuition. 2. clear understanding of the inner nature of some specific thing. 3. a) Psychological Awareness of one's own mental attitudes and behavior, b) Psychiatry recognition of one's own mental disorder.

(1) Agreement with your actions in substance abuse/behavior.

(2) Understanding into what makes your actions different from others.

(3) Insight into your remorse, acceptance of responsibility, and understanding over WHY the need to abuse drugs /alcohol or behavior issues.

Even though Insight is a very subjective thing to prove and it may give others the opportunity to pick apart your statements without citing specific facts. It is very important from a recovery stand point that you can explore, cite, and understand the causative factors of your substance abuse.

The reasons can be as varied as the substances that are available. But, an example of those reasons can include but are not limited to the following:

1. Bad choices.

2. Normalizing substance abuse/ behavior through previous encounters with other family member's using, and stating "everyone else is doing it," or "just one more time."

3. Anger and impulse control issues.

4. The direct action before and after intoxication and drug use.

5. Low self-esteem and depression.

6. Peer pressure and poor personal associations

These are just a few of the many reasons a life of substance abuse can occur. Your job is to be able to list and detail whatever reasons apply to why your life is controlled by substance abuse.

Lastly, you have to share INSIGHT into your understanding of the effect and impact of your substance abuse. Invariably, there are many people that are hurt by your substance abuse. This means those directly affected and those that are indirectly affected. Being able to openly discuss the impact it has and will continue to have with your actions is crucial to becoming aware of what needs to change in your life style.

It must be understood that substance abuse has literally an unfathomable amount of victims because when the use starts from the farmer (manufacture) of the substance, it affects people that the abuser has never met, and this continues to the day that one over-doses and the people are affected in the medical and psychological care of the abuser at this point.

_____
_____
_____
_____
_____
_____
_____
_____
_____
_____
_____
_____
_____
_____
_____
_____
_____

Pathway to an *Addictive Free* Lifestyle

PERSONAL DEVELOPMENT ASSIGNMENT

WEEK TWO

FEAR BASED OR LOVE BASED LIVE STYLE

You will read the following, several times if necessary, and then write a short statement dealing with how you are living life. Which is it, a 'FEAR BASED' or a 'LOVE BASED' life style?

Let us look at how the 'Sobriety and Wellness' describes the two (2) thought systems concerning 'Love Based' and 'Fear Based' thinking.

Therefore, our thinking will be in only one of two thought systems. One we call LOVE and the other we call FEAR. The system called 'Love' is where the culture was developed. This is where ceremonies are born, where songs are developed, and where we learned to pray. Here are some examples of characteristics in these systems.

'Love-Based' Thought Systems:

Unity	Balance	Respect	Forgiveness
Love-Seeker	Honor	Honesty	Justice
Responsible	Patience	Acceptance	

'Power-with … People, places, and things'!

"Fear-Based' Thought Systems:

Conflict	Fault Finder	Disrespect	Irresponsible
Dishonest	Malicious Teasing	Shame	Guilt
Sarcasm	Belittling	Anger	Control
Impatience			

'Power over … People, place, and things!'

During our substance abuse we live in the 'Fear-Based' thought system of negative people and one that has caused endless unhappiness to ourselves and those close to us. When we drink, use drugs we are negative people living in a 'Fear-Based' thought system.

The 'Fear-Based' thought system is also called an ego thought system. 'EGO' is a word that means 'I' in a negative term. It means 'too much of me.' It means that I am self-centered and acting as if no one else exists. It means I am selfish and full of anger and fear. All of us are this way when we are drinking and using drugs. We may also feel that way in the early days / stages of our recovery.

As negative people we tend to be 'attackers, fault finders and very judgmental people.' We feel guilty and will use words of guilt to shame other people. Our words will be sarcastic and belitting. We are always concerned with looking good in the eyes of others and being Mr. or Ms. RIGHT.

Being in the ego or fear system, we are constantly seeking power over people, places, and things. We must be in control. And we probably thrive on excitement and chaos. If you recognize yourself in this description, it might mean you have the honesty to work these concepts.

Now, let us look at the positive people. They are grounded in the 'Love-Based' through system. Our traditional societies were deeply rooted in positive ideas. That doesn't mean that they were all saints or perfect people. It just means that when individuals got off center, the people as a whole were the role models to bring them back into perspective. Positive people feel a great deal of unity, harmony, and balance in their lives. They feel a great deal of respect and are able to forgive when injustices are done to them. They are men and women of honor and integrity.

Complete the Personal Development Assignment with the above stated information, by writing a short statement about how 'fear controlled your lifestyle during your substance abuse and poor behavior.'

(3). The Red Road to 'Sobriety and Wellness'; in the Native Way, White Bison, Inc. 2002.

_____
_____
_____
_____
_____
_____
_____
_____
_____
_____

GROUP DISCUSSION

WEEK TWO

SESSION 2

ANALYZING VICTIMIZATION

This group discussion will look into Victimization: Your Victim(s), Self, Family, Community, and Society. First, we need to establish that this is your community and society. The people you care about live here. What happens here, affects your family and yourself, therefore, this is YOUR COMMUNITY. Even though your perception may be that it is not. Who is really affected by the world of substance abuse? What are the aspects to oneself, family, and the community and society at large? The group is given guidance into how to stop the cycle of victimization and introduce this concept into their Life-Plan.

DISCUSSION QUESTIONS

1. Let us discuss who is really hurt directly by substance abuse or negative behavior.

   _____
   _____
   _____

2. Let us discuss how you have become your own victim.

   _____
   _____
   _____

3. Let us discuss how you and others have made your family a victim.

   _____
   _____
   _____

Now, what has the substance abuse or negative behavior caused to your community and to society as a whole?

Keep this information in your own mind while doing your personal Development Assignment. This will give you better insight on what are the consequences of your actions and which made you start abusing any substance.

_____
_____
_____
_____
_____
_____
_____
_____
_____
_____
_____
_____
_____
_____
_____
_____
_____
_____
_____
_____

Pathway to an *Addiction Free* Lifestyle

PERSONAL DEVELOPMENT ASSIGNMENT

WEEK TWO

INTRODUCTION TO THE LIFE PLAN

Name: _____

Life Plan outline: GOALS

1. Short Term Goals:

    a) One Week
    b) One Month
    c) Six Months
    d) One Year

    Example: I want to make sure I run at least five (5) miles this week.
    I want to read three (3) books this month.
    My goal for the next six (6) months is not to use drugs.

2. Long Term Goals:

    a) Eighteen Months
    b) Two Years
    c) Three Years
    d) Five Years

LIFE PLAN ACTION STEPS:

You must begin your Life-Plan outline now. While constructing your Life-Plan make sure you consider what resources that it will take to complete them. So honestly assess all aspects of what it will take to complete them.

Pathway to an *Addictive Free* Lifestyle

WEEK TWO

INTRODUCTION TO THE LIFE PLAN

Name: _____

Life Plan outline: GOALS

1. **Short Term Goals:**

    A. One Week

    _____

    _____

    B. One Month

    _____

    _____

    C. Six Months

    _____

    _____

    D. One Year

    _____

    _____

Example: I want to make sure I run at least five (5) miles this week.

I want to read three (3) books this month.

My goal for the next six (6) months is not to use drugs.

2. **Long Term Goals:**

    A. Eighteen Months

    _____

B. Two Years

C. Three Years

D. Five Years

LIFE PLAN ACTION STEPS:

You must begin your Life-Plan outline now. While constructing your Life-Plan make sure you consider what resources that it will take to complete them. So honestly assess all aspect of what it will take to complete them.

Pathway to an *Addiction Free* Lifestyle

GROUP DISCUSSION

WEEK TWO

SESSION 3

12-STEP VERSES GROUP THERAPY

The group discussion will give an understanding to the difference between the 12-Step style and the group therapy style and why we are combining them.

Historically, a certain opposition has existed between the proponents of these two (2) modalities, with subtle and at times overt denigration of one another.

So, when individuals abuse substances they typically experience substantial interpersonal disturbance at every stage of their illness. When dealing with emotional pain that the individual attempts to abate by substance abuse; they have relational difficulties resulting from the substance abuse; 2) they have interpersonal difficulties that complicate the maintenance of sobriety. We must take into account there are over one-hundred types/styles of 12-Step programs but the most prevalent and popular is Alcoholics Anonymous Program.

Group Therapy and 12-Step can complement one another if certain obstacles are removed. The trained counselors will understand the mechanism of the 12-Step work group, and support those who have their struggles of recovery within this system. One (1) major aspect of the 12-Step system is that it's members' rely heavily on the relationship to a higher power, the submission to that power, and the understanding of the 'self' in relation to the higher power.

Group Therapy encourages member-to-member interaction, especially in the here-and-now: it is the lifeblood of the group. 12-Step, by contrast, specially prohibits 'cross talk,' which is the direct interaction between members during a meeting. Cross talk must be understood that it could be any direct inquiry, suggestion, advice, feedback, or criticism.

With all this in mind, how do we integrate this knowledge into the Life Plan.

Example:	First we show how the group and the 12-Step program need to be utilized together and separately to maximize the potential for a successful 'Recovery and Social Wellness' life style. So, in your Life Plan place in areas and times that you will attend said named programs and how this support system has short- and long-term affects while it keeps the effective relapse prevention steps in place. This method strengthens your insight into your substance abuse.
Example:	Go to work from 8:30AM-to-Noon. At lunch stop by the civic center to a 12-Step study while I eat my lunch. Finish off the day with working my Step. After

work, at 6:00PM I will go to a Group Therapy for an hour and discuss my Life Plan and if anything is stopping me from completing my weekly goals, etc.

Insight is not an exact science. Recovery comes when you are genuine about the details you share when reviewing your life of substance abuse. These are aspects of your recovery and are on the road to 'Recovery and Social Wellness'. Once again having Insight each individual will come to a point in which the addict understands that substance abuse is only the result of a bigger problem or an underlining problem or reason for the need to use drugs/alcohol.

_____
_____
_____
_____
_____
_____
_____
_____
_____
_____
_____
_____
_____
_____
_____
_____
_____
_____
_____

Pathway to an *Addiction Free* Lifestyle
PERSONAL DEVELOPMENT ASSIGNMENT

WEEK TWO

12-STEP VERSES GROUP THERAPY

These Five Stages of Recovery must be outlined so each individual will understand where they are in their stage of recovery. This is how to integrate and apply this knowledge within the 12-Step process.

Stage 1   **Pre-contemplation:** A stage of change in which the individual may wish to change but either lacks the serious intention to undergo change in the foreseeable future or is unaware of how significant his/her problem has become.

Stage 2   **Contemplation:** A stage in which the individual is aware that a problem exist and is thinking about overcoming it but has not yet made a commitment to take action.

Stage 3   **Preparation:** A stage of change in which the individual seriously considers taking action to overcome a problem within the next thirty (30) days and has unsuccessfully taken action over the past twelve (12) months.

Stage 4   **Action:** A stage of change in which the individual actually modifies his/her behavior and environment to overcome a problem.

Stage 5   **Maintenance:** A stage in which the individual has not experienced problems related to substance use and maintains awareness that relapse can happen, and to extend recovery to other areas of one's life style.

These are very simple examples of how to combine the two (2) different systems of recovery into your Life Plan and the short- and long-term goals. Please do not limit your ideas or options for only long-term recovery.

Irwin D. Yalom. The Theory and Practice of Group Psychotherapy. 5th Ed. R. Metans and I. Yalom. International Journal of Group Psychotherapy 4th Ed (1991): 269-93

Pathway to an *Addiction Free* Lifestyle

PERSONAL DEVELOPMENT ASSIGNMENT

WEEK TWO

INTRODUCTION TO THE LIFE PLAN

Complete Personal Development Assignment by using the group discussion on Stages of recovery, 12-Step and Group Processes, and write out several ideas on how to integrate these concepts into your Life Plan.

_____
_____
_____
_____
_____
_____
_____
_____
_____
_____
_____
_____
_____
_____

WEEK THREE

Learning Objective

- ❖ Principles, Laws and Values
- ❖ Anger: What it is and what it is not
- ❖ Self-talk, Perceptions and Reality Model
- ❖ 24 Hour Goal
- ❖ Self Awareness
- ❖ Culture Identity and Drug Use

Pathway to an *Addiction Free* Lifestyle

GROUP DISCUSSION

WEEK THREE

SESSION 1

PRINCIPLES, LAWS, AND VALUES

The group discussion will be dealing with the concepts of Principles, Laws, and Values. What they are and why they are important during our journey of 'Recovery and Social Wellness'. We must remember to change our way of thinking, since our best thinking at the time sent us to a 'life' of misery whether it be for a 'life sentence,' or doing 'life on the installment plan.' What is a Principle? Let us look at the dictionary's definition. PRINCIPLE: 1. the ultimate source, origin or cause of something; 2. a fundamental truth, law, doctrine or motivating force, upon which others are based; 3. a rule of conduct. So as it relates to this issue of substance abuse it is what is most important to the addict. The addict lives by the principle that drugs/alcohol and an altered state of mind is more important than anything else i.e.; the getting, then the using, then getting more (to use) is the most important objective of their life. We have to change our principle thinking into the most important which is to become clean and sober. If the addict put half the effort into a job as they do into getting, by any means, into an altered state, they could make a very good living. Show examples of how it can be done.

What is a Law? Let us look at the dictionary's definition. LAW: Something laid down or settled; 1) all the rules of conduct established and enforced by the authority, legislation, or custom of a given community, state, or other group. 2) the condition existing when obedience to such rules is general. This is very true to the substance abuse life style. For example: How many times has it been stated 'Street Rules;' Rules of the Jungle;' etc. The addict is just living by the laws of his group or other addicts as they do crimes to obtain their substance of choice. Now we must show by example how the Laws of the community at large are more important than the substance they are abusing. Why should they live by the Laws set down by people they do not care about or they feel care about them.

What are values? Let us look at the dictionary's definition. VALUES: to be strong; 6) that which is desirable or worthy of esteem for its own sake, thing or quality having intrinsic worth. 7) the social principles, goals, or standard held or accepted by an individual, class, society, etc. Using this understanding: since most addicts have very little value for not only themselves but for anyone else they put the most value on the substance of their choice.

Living by Principles, Laws, and Values that are surrounded by 'stinking thinking' of substance abuse becomes a cycle of hurt and destruction. When we are turning our life around and being clean and sober for any length of time clearer thinking starts and the addict can focus on a path to understanding what is more important. Breaking the cycle of hurt and living in harmony with all that is around us brings balance to our life.

Pathway to an *Addiction Free* Lifestyle

PERSONAL DEVELOPMENT ASSIGNMENT

WEEK THREE

ANGER MANAGEMENT

For this Development Assignment, answer the following questions, in your own words. Especially focus on how anger may affect others in your life and how uncontrolled anger leads back to substance abuse.

1. What is anger?

   _____
   _____
   _____
   _____
   _____

2. How has anger and aggression effected your life?

   _____
   _____
   _____
   _____
   _____

3. What causes anger and what causes your anger?

   _____
   _____
   _____
   _____

4. How can you manage your anger? Give three (3) examples.

_____

_____

_____

_____

_____

5. How does uncontrolled anger lead back to substance abuse?

_____

_____

_____

_____

_____

Pathway to an *Addiction Free* Lifestyle

GROUP DISCUSSION

WEEK THREE

SESSION 2

SELF-TALK, PERCEPTION AND THE REALITY MODEL

The group discussion will give each individual the ability to recognize Self-Talk, Perceptions, and what it is going to take to treat these areas in our life to help with your 'Recovery and Social Wellness'. These areas of growth and Self-Talk include the emotional, the mental, the physical, and the spiritual.

When individuals are listening, mostly they are talking to themselves so the perception of what the other person is trying to express gets turned around. Preconditioned cultural beliefs are ideas of concepts we hold to be true. The Self-Talk cycle is the constant conversation we have with ourselves about what is happening to us and around us. However, we do not store and record the 'truth:' what we store and record is 'the truth as we see it.' So if we decide to change or grow, this self-image becomes a major barrier to change. See: A Cognitive Reality Model.

The power of words on the self-image is amazing. That is why it is so important to become aware of how we talk to ourselves and others, and how others talk to us.

_____

_____

_____

_____

_____

_____

_____

_____

_____

_____

Pathway to an *Addiction Free* Lifestyle
GROUP DISCUSSION / PERSONAL DEVELOPMENT ASSIGNMENT

WEEK THREE

SESSION 2

BARRIERS TO CHANGE

*"Whether you think you can
or think you can't, you're right."*

Henry Ford

SUMMARY OF KEY CONCEPTS

In this session, we will discuss how our Habits / Habitual Behaviors and our Attitudes can be barriers when they no longer fit our changing paradigm. We will also discuss how the way we talk to ourselves and what we believe to be true controls our performance, and, ultimately, our lives.

LEARNING OBJECTIVES:

By the end of this session, we should all have an understanding of the following:

1. How our habits and attitudes can be barriers in the change process.

2. The role of our self-talk in creating our self-image.

CONCEPTS

HABITS / HABITUAL BEHAVIOR:

Habitual behavior is automatic behavior. Habits are necessary because they allow us to do several things at the same time. Most of the time our habitual behavior is helpful, but some habits can be barriers or obstacles. To the extent that we have been conditioned or programmed to think and act habitually, we may fall into the trap of trying to use old irrelevant habits to deal with new experiences and challenges.

Thinking patterns can become habits. An example would be of giving up accountability, saying "it's not my fault," and fixing the blame on a bad lawyer, a bad judge, and "they" and "them." A habit to give up accountability for everything.

ATTITUDES:

Attitudes are subconscious habits—they are the way you lean on the subconscious level. If you lean toward and seek things out, you are said to have a positive attitudes about it. If you lean away and avoid something, you are said to have a negative attitude about it. Attitudes are developed through knowledge or experience with emotional impact. Many times, we accept attitudes from other people. These attitudes can be about ourselves, about others, and about situations, we have never experienced. If we want to make changes in our lives, it is necessary to look at the attitudes we have that might limit us, recognize attitudes that are no longer working for us, and make a conscious commitment to change those attitudes in order to reach our vision.

SELF-TALK CYCLE:

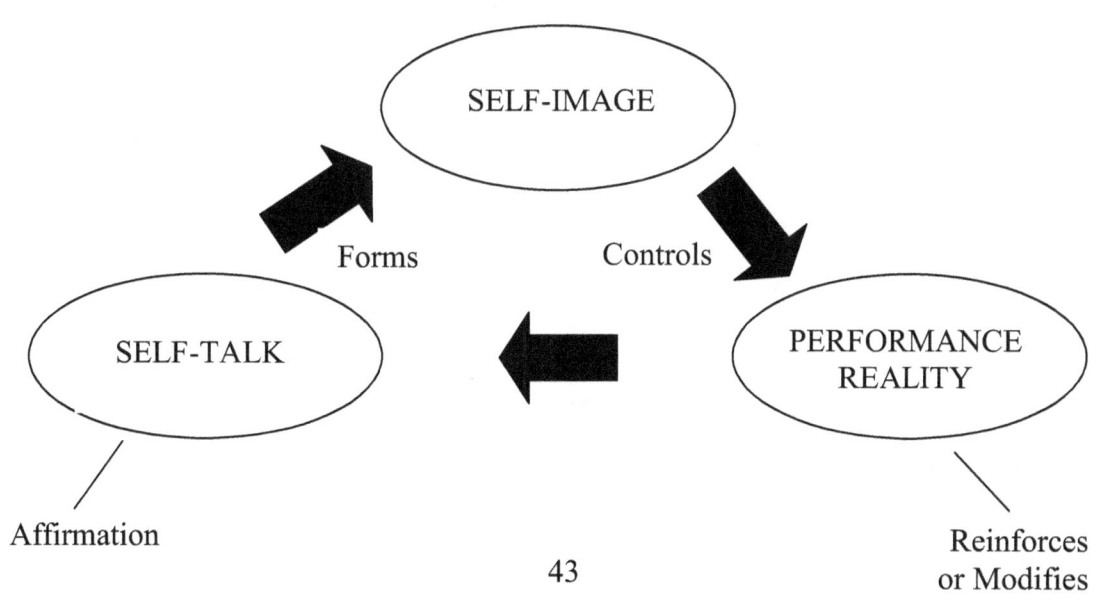

The self-talk cycle is the constant conversation we have with ourselves about what is happening to us and around us. However, we don't store and record the "truth," we store and record the "truth" as we see it. So if we decide to change or grow, this self-image becomes a major barrier to change.

Our present thoughts determine our future. If we change the way we think, we change the way we act! We move toward what we think about ... and we usually think about what we don't want.

This is one of the most important concepts we can understand. We all tend to focus on what we don't want. We think about the problem rather than the solution. Where are you spending time in your mind? Is your self-talk leading you toward what you want in life, or toward what you don't want?

24-HOUR CHALLENGE

The power of words on the self-image is amazing. That is why it is so important to become aware of how we talk to others, and ourselves and how others talk to us.

For the next 24 hours, make a decision to not put yourself or others down. Don't participate in any sarcasm, ridicule, or put-downs. Negative thinking is a habit, and the alcohol / drug culture can be one of the most negative environments there is.

(Ref. A Framework for Breaking Barriers)

Pathway to an *Addiction Free* Lifestyle

GROUP DISCUSSION

WEEK THREE

SESSION 2

A principle/belief is internal.

A habit is the acting out of a principle/belief

An attitude is the external expression of a principle/belief

An expression is a principle/belief projected into the future.

HABITS/HABITUAL BEHAVIOR:

List the most significant habit you use each day.

_____
_____
_____
_____

Is that habit a barrier or obstacle in your life? Why?

_____
_____
_____
_____

ATTITUDES:

Is your current attitude: (circle one)

    A. Positive

    B. Negative

    C. Both

If your attitude is positive, explain how you plan to use it to change your life.

_____

_____

_____

_____

If your attitude is negative, explain how that negativity acts as a barrier towards change.

_____

_____

_____

_____

If you exhibit both positive and negative attitudes, explain which one is more dominate, and how the two competing attitudes affect your life.

_____

_____

_____

_____

Pathway to an *Addiction Free* Lifestyle

PERSONAL DEVELOPMENT ASSIGNMENT

WEEK THREE

24-HOUR GOAL

The goal is for the next 24-hours only positive thoughts and expressions. Then on a separate piece of paper, write down the instances what and when you express anything negative, whether it was a thought or you actually said something to another person. Be open and honest with this exercise.

_____
_____
_____
_____
_____
_____
_____
_____
_____
_____
_____
_____
_____

Pathway to an *Addiction Free* Lifestyle

GROUP DISCUSSION

WEEK THREE

SESSION 3

SELF-AWARENESS

IDENTITY OF SELF VERSUS OUTSIDE PERCEPTIONS

The group discussion will cover the Self-Awareness aspect. Start the discussion by describing yourself to the group then put some of the participants on the spot by choosing two (2) of them and ask them to describe themselves to the group. Then turn it around and ask someone else in the group to give their perception of the person that just described themselves. By doing this it will give each person the ability to start understanding how others look at them or think of what their perception is. That type of insight gives each individual the difference between their truth and what are others' perceptions.

A lot of times our actions take on a life because we think or feel others may think of us as one way when we are not. So, having the ability to express who we are to others starts to open up different ideas and cultural identity's.

As for the Personal Development Assignment have the group write down how they perceive their individual culture with substance abuse. Also add a short paragraph on what others' view their perceptions of their culture and their substance abuse is.

> Example: The usual statement concerning alcohol is; 'do not give it to Indians as they go crazy.' But how does the Indian look at him / her-self concerning these issues.

How does it feel to think about substance abuse and one's cultural identity? In five sentences, on the lines below, explain what substances were accepted in your culture.

_____

_____

_____

_____

_____

_____

_____

Pathway to an *Addiction Free* Lifestyle
PERSONAL DEVELOPMENT ASSIGNMENT

WEEK THREE

CULTURE, IDENTITY AND DRUG USE

For this Personal Development Assignment, on the lines below, you will be writing a half-page analysis of how you perceive your individual culture and how substance abuse is connected in anyway. Then a short paragraph on how you think others' perceive your culture and substance abuse.

_____
_____
_____
_____
_____
_____
_____
_____
_____
_____
_____
_____
_____
_____
_____
_____
_____

WEEK FOUR

Learning Objective

- ❖ View Point: Path of Destruction
- ❖ Human Body and Effects of Substance Abuse
- ❖ Communication of One's Own Self Awareness and Reality Model Revisited
- ❖ Over the Counter verses Street Substance Abuse
- ❖ Short and Long-Term Damage to the Body by Substance Abuse
- ❖ Substance Abuse Damages to the Human Body

Pathway to an *Addiction Free* Lifestyle

GROUP DISCUSSION

WEEK FOUR

SESSION 1

VIEWPOINT: PATH OF DESTRUCTION

In this group discussion we will trace our decision making history, both functional and dysfunctional. This will be done in a sincere effort to segregate former maladaptive behaviors. We must isolate and examine the causes and affects these decisions have had on our past life cycle. Analyzing and exploring alternate decisions making processes to uncover the presenting problems that may have lead to our personal path of destruction.

The following is a list of what type of affect those specific substances have had on your body's functioning system.

Let us take a close look at the toxicity of popular drugs. "Both the physical or psychological harm that a drug might present to the user." (Drugs, Behavior, and Modern Society 7th Ed.)

    Acute Toxicity: the physical or psychological harm a drug might present to the user immediately or soon after the drug is ingested into the body.

    Chronic Toxicity: the physical or psychological harm a drug might cause over a long period of use.

    Tolerance and Behavioral Tolerance: the process of drug tolerance that is linked to drug taking behavior occurring consistently in the same surroundings under the same circumstances, also known as conditional tolerance.

A number of important issues with respect to drug taking behavior will be examined. What exactly are the problems associated with chronic drug use? What are the various diseases caused by substance abuse toxicity, (a drug's ability to damage biological systems)?

The following are just a short list of examples of affects of certain common substances:

    ALCOHOL: Alcohol induced dementia; uncoordinated motor skills; unpredictable states of disinhibition. More serious ailments include liver damage (Cirrhosis) and the destruction of nerve cells, Pancreatitis which in itself can cause many different diseases such as diabetes, and recurrent intestinal tract infections.

    TOBACCO: Cardiovascular disease, a narrowing and clotting of the coronary arteries. Pulmonary disease, labored breathing, chest pain, increased susceptibility to infections of the respiratory tract, and Emphysema (a form of irreversible lung damage).

MARIJUANA (Cannabis Sativa): Increased heart rate increased blood pressure similar to tobacco but contains more tars, and immunosuppressant dangers.

COCAINE/CRACK: Low-moderate usage: Alertness; hyperactivity; increased body temperature; pupillatory dilation; and blood flow shift from internal organs to the muscles.

Chronic usage: Hemorrhagic strokes; seizures; inter-cranial hemorrhaging; heart attack(s); infections of the heart; pulmonary edema; bronchialitis; ulcers; intestinal infraction and renal failure. Paranoid psychosis that may last for hours at a time.

HEROIN: Several withdrawal symptoms and the possibility of an incurable neurological disease in which a progressive loss of muscle coordination can lead to paralyses and death as well as kidney degeneration.

METHAMPHETAMINE/ICE: Affects are very much like those of cocaine, except for Ice where the paranoid psychosis may persist for days, if not weeks.

ECSTASY: Can cause malignant hypothermia which includes disorientation, convulsions, the breakdown of muscle and skeletal loss, kidney failure, cardiac arrhythmias, necrosis of the brain and also death.

These are very short descriptions on these substances that will give you the idea of what is the long-term affects which re-enforces the old statement that 'Jails, Institutions, and Death' is the road taken with drug usage. Addicts may know the effects since that is what they are seeking, but the early death process is a very painful way to go.

_____

_____

_____

_____

_____

_____

Pathway to an *Addiction Free* Lifestyle

PERSONAL DEVELOPMENT ASSIGNMENT

WEEK FOUR

THE HUMAN BODY AND THE EFFECTS OF SUBSTANCE ABUSE

For this handout you must read and be able to discuss the Hepatitis handout. Answer the questions on handout H-21, also be prepared to openly discuss all the different aspects of substance abuse and emotional contents of the abuse. Write a page on the affects and treatment of the Hepatitis and the HIV viruses.

_____
_____
_____
_____
_____
_____
_____
_____
_____
_____
_____
_____
_____
_____
_____

Pathway to an *Addiction Free* Lifestyle

GROUP DISCUSSION

WEEK FOUR

SESSION 2

THE REALITY MODEL

This group discussion will focus on the Reality Model as stated in Breaking Barriers Phase II, by Gordon Graham. Addiction is compulsive behavior with short-term benefits and long-term destruction. So we look at the natural laws and do the exercises that will fulfill the basic ideas of how we look at human needs and our belief system. Let us review 65-76, and discuss. (4) Breaking Barriers, Gordon Graham, 1998, Cognitive Reality Model

_____
_____
_____
_____
_____
_____
_____
_____
_____
_____
_____
_____
_____
_____
_____

Pathway to an *Addiction Free* Lifestyle

GROUP DISCUSSION / PERSONNAL DEVELOPMENT ASSIGNMENT

WEEK FOUR

SESSION 2

THE REALITY MODEL

> *"The most trifling actions of a man ...*
> *give a nice observer some notion of his mind."*
> Benjamin Franklin

SUMMARY OF KEY CONCEPTS

In this session, we will discuss the Reality Model. This discussion will help us understand how to use the model in our own lives.

LEARNING OBJECTIVES:

1. A deeper understanding of how our principles drive behavior.

2. Evaluating the results of our behavior based on long-term success.

3. The importance of identifying faulty principles on our belief window.

Pathway to an *Addiction Free* Lifestyle

CONCEPTS

Addiction is compulsive behavior with short-term benefits and long-term destruction.

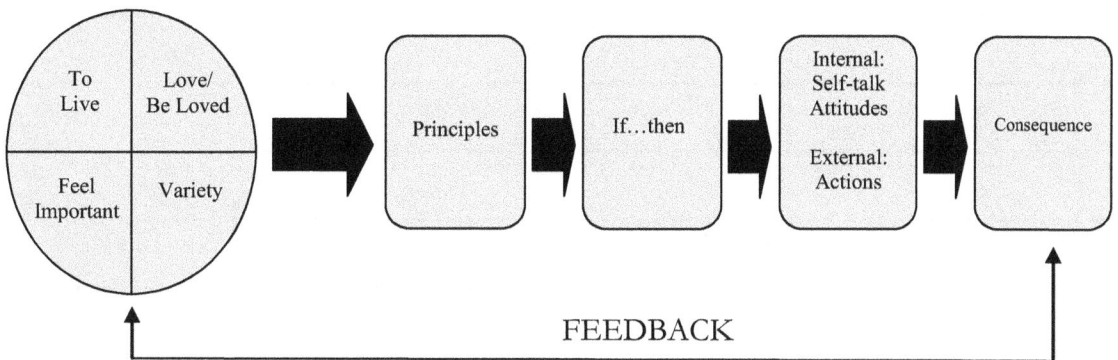

Will the results of my behavior meet my needs over time?

NATURAL LAWS:

1. If the results of your behavior do not meet your needs over time, you have an incorrect principle on your belief window.

2. Results take time to measure.

GROUP DISCUSSION

      To Live ...
      To love and be loved ...
      To feel important ...
      To have variety ...

1. What are the most common addictions among men and women?

_____

_____

2. Identify three addictions that have had a negative influence on your life.

_____

_____

Pathway to an *Addiction Free* Lifestyle

PERSONAL DEVELOPMENT ASSIGNMENT

WEEK FOUR

OVER THE COUNTER VERSUS STREET SUBSTANCE ABUSE

This Personal Development Assignment will cover over-the-counter drugs, prescription drugs, and their contrast to illicit drug abuse.

Prescription drugs are medicinal drugs available to the public only when approved by a medical professional and dispensed by a licensed pharmacist.

Over-the-counter drugs are medicinal drugs available to the public without a prescription and they are often referred to as non-prescription drugs.

Illicit drugs are drugs whose manufacture, sale, or possession is illegal.

What are the specific risks and dangers of specific drugs? We must explain the standards of the Food & Drug Administration (FDA). So, some may argue the FDA is just a melting pot for drug companies which may be true or not, so for the sake of this discussion the over-the-counter drugs have gone through a very long 'vetting' process which includes quality control and consumer safety issues. The street illicit drugs are manufactured in all sorts of different, untested, unsafe environments by non-professional personnel. This leads to a very unsafe substance. This can change the strength and the effect of the drug while remaining in the same volume. This is what has lead to many deaths by accidental overdose. This is especially true when combining the over-the-counter drugs with illicit substances.

For this Personal Development Assignment you must write what you feel the difference between the two (2) are and what types of substances did you use and combine during your substance abuse journey.

_____

_____

_____

_____

_____

_____

_____

_____

Pathway to an *Addiction Free* Lifestyle
GROUP DISCUSSION

WEEK FOUR

SESSION 3

SHORT- and LONG-TERM DAMAGE TO BODY BY SUBSTANCE ABUSE

This group discussion will look into the aspects of how alcohol and other chemical substance have short- and long-term effects on the body.

Pharmacokinetic, is how drugs are handled by the body.

(A primer of drug action, Robert m. Julien, Claire D. Advokat, and Joseph E. Comaty. 12th Ed. Chap 1). They give a basic example by the taking (ingesting of aspirin).

1. <u>Absorption</u>: the aspirin is absorbed into the body by swallowing a tablet.

2. <u>Distribution</u>: of the aspirin throughout the body, including into a fetus if a female patient is pregnant at the time the drug is ingested.

3. <u>Metabolism (detoxification or breakdown)</u>: of the drug as the aspirin that has exerted its analgesic effect is broken down into metabolites (by-product or waste products) that no longer exert any effects.

4. <u>Elimination</u>: of the metabolic waste products, usually in the urine. (See figure 1.1 from the 12th ED 2010).

As we look at the figure 1.1 on page 75, the schematic representation of the fate of a drug in the body whether it is by intra-muscular intravenous; trans-membrane; subcutaneous; or smoked (inhaled). Now we have to compare what type of substance in which we abused and understand how much damage could have been done over this time line to your body.

OVER THE COUNTER VERSUS STREET SUBSTANCE ABUSE

This Personal Development Assignment will cover over-the-counter drugs, prescription drugs, and their contrast to illicit drug abuse.

Prescription drugs are medicinal drugs available to the public only when approved by a medical professional and dispensed by a licensed pharmacist.

Over-the-counter drugs are medicinal drugs available to the public without a prescription and they are often referred to as non-prescription drugs.

Pathway to an *Addiction Free* Lifestyle

GROUP DISCUSSION

WEEK FOUR

SESSION 3

PHARMACOKINETICS: is the study of what the body does to a drug.

The root kinetics in the word pharmacokinetics implies movement and time. The focus of pharmacokinetics is on the time course of the drug's movement through the body, particularly its half-life and any complications that arise from alterations in its rate of metabolism.

When we have a headache, we take it for granted that after taking some aspirin our headache will probably disappear within 15 to 30 minutes. We also take it for granted that, unless we take more aspirin later, the headache may recur within 3 or 4 hours. This familiar scenario illustrates the four basic processes in pharmacokinetics. Using the aspirin example, the four processes are as follows:

1. ***Absorption*** of the aspirin into the body from the swallowed tablet

2. ***Distribution*** of the aspirin throughout the body, including into the fetus if a female patient is pregnant at the time the drug is taken

3. ***Metabolism*** (detoxification or breakdown) of the drug as the aspirin that has exerted its analgesic effect is broken down into metabolites (by-products or waste products) that no longer exert any effect

4. ***Elimination*** of the metabolic waste products, usually in the urine

These four processes in concert, determine how much of the drug that is administered actually reaches its target. The understanding of pharmacokinetics, along with knowledge about the dosage taken, allows determination of the concentration of a drug at its sites of action (receptors), and the intensity of drug effect on the receptors as a function of time.

Pharmacokinetics in its simplest form describes the time course of a particular drug's actions and the time to onset and the duration of effect. The time course simply reflects the amount of time required for the rise and fall of the drug's concentration at the target site. Figure 1.1 illustrates the complexity of drug movement through the body and its equilibrium at its site of action.

Pathway to an *Addiction Free* Lifestyle

GROUP DISCUSSION

WEEK FOUR

SESSION 3

Now, knowing the fate of a drug in the body, let's review the discussion from week four--session one on the effects of specific drugs within the body.

ALCOHOL: Alcohol induced dementia; uncoordinated motor skills; unpredictable states of disinhibition. More serious ailments include liver damage (Cirrhosis) and the destruction of nerve cells, Pancreatitis which in itself can cause many different diseases such as diabetes, and recurrent intestinal tract infections.

TOBACCO: Cardiovascular disease, a narrowing and clotting of the coronary arteries. Pulmonary disease, labored breathing, chest pain, increased susceptibility to infections of the respiratory tract, and Emphysema (a form of irreversible lung damage).

COCAINE/CRACK: Low-moderate usage: Alertness; hyperactivity; increased body temperature; pupillatory dilation; and blood flow shift from internal organs to the muscles.

Chronic usage: Hemorrhagic strokes; seizures; inter-cranial hemorrhaging; heart attack(s); infections of the heart; pulmonary edema; bronchialitis; ulcers; intestinal infraction and renal failure. Paranoid psychosis that may last for hours at a time.

HEROIN: Several withdrawal symptoms and the possibility of an incurable neurological disease in which a progressive loss of muscle coordination can lead to paralyses and death as well as kidney degeneration.

METHAMPHETAMINE/ICE: Affects are very much like those of cocaine, except for Ice where the paranoid psychosis may persist for days, if not weeks.

ECSTASY: Can cause malignant hypothermia which includes disorientation, convulsions, the breakdown of muscle and skeletal loss, kidney failure, cardiac arrhythmias, necrosis of the brain and also death.

MARIJUANA (Cannabis Sativa): Increased heart rate increased blood pressure similar to tobacco but contains more tars, and immunosuppressant dangers.

Pathway to an *Addiction Free* Lifestyle

GROUP DISCUSSION

WEEK FOUR

SESSION 3

What was your drug of choice?

( ) ALCOHOL   ( ) TOBACCO   ( ) COCAINE/CRACK   ( ) HEROIN

( ) METHAMPHETAMINE/ICE   ( ) ECSTASY   ( ) MARUJUANA

List the short-term damage from using this drug

_____
_____
_____
_____

List the long-term damage from using this drug.

_____
_____
_____
_____

Referring to the Figure 1.1 handout how was the drug of your choice ingested?

( ) ORALLY   ( ) INJECTED   ( ) INHALED   ( ) SNORTED   ( ) TRANSDERMAL

Which rout is the quickest way to the site of action?

_____
_____
_____

If you have never used or experimented with drugs or alcohol, what addiction or behavior led to your path of destruction?

_____

_____

_____

_____

List the short-term and long-term damage this addiction or behavior has had on your body. Short-term damage:

_____

_____

_____

_____

Long-term damage:

_____

_____

_____

_____

Pathway to an *Addiction Free* Lifestyle

GROUP DISCUSSION

WEEK FOUR

SESSION 3

ABSORPTION

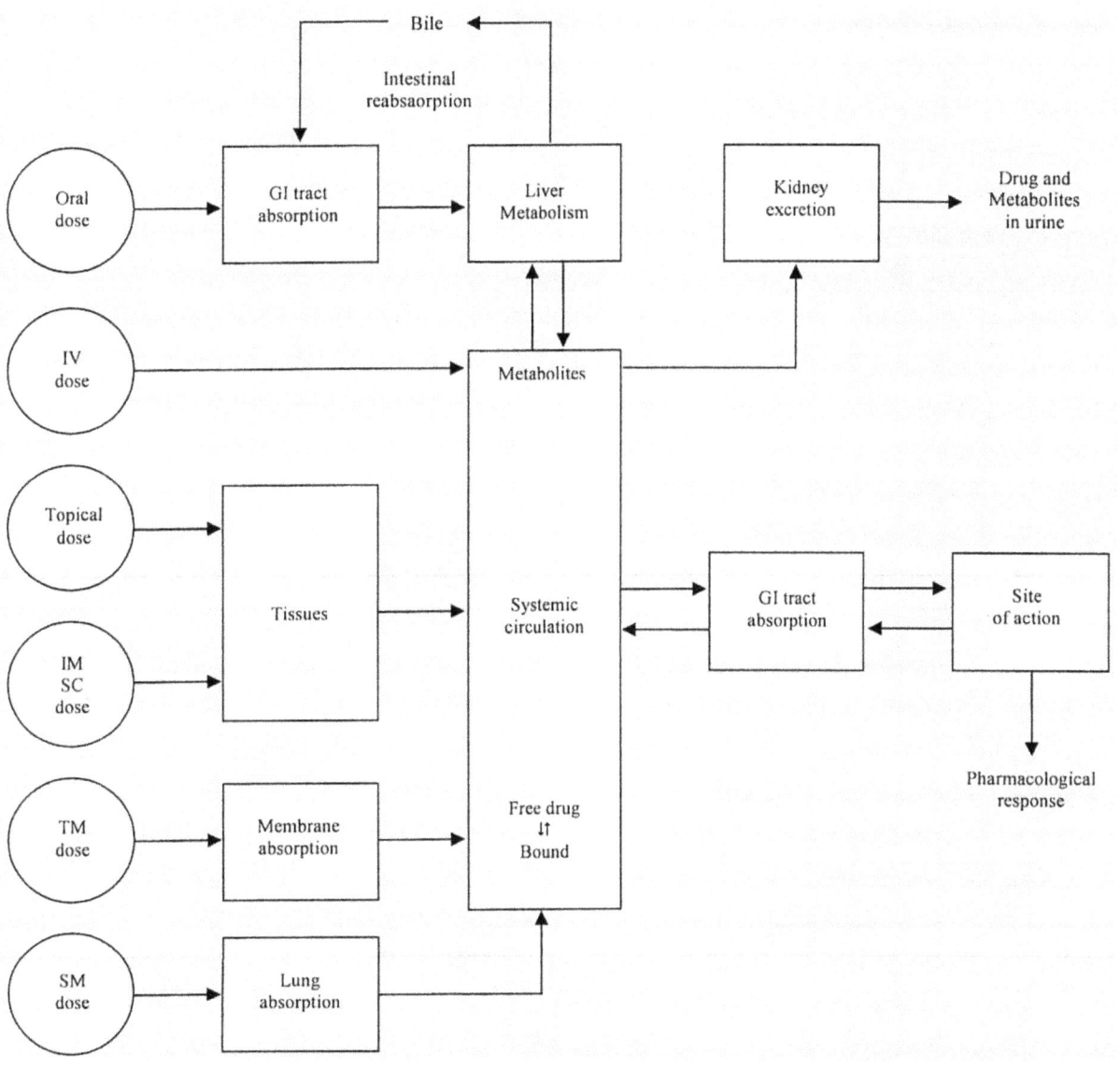

FIGURE 1.1 Schematic representation of the fate of a drug in the body: IM = intramuscular; IV = intravenous; TM = transmembrane; SC = subcutaneous; SM = smoked.

Pathway to an *Addiction Free* Lifestyle

PERSONAL DEVELOPMENT

ASSIGNMENT

WEEK FOUR

SUBSTANCE ABUSES DAMAGE TO THE HUMAN BODY

This Personal Development Assignment will require you to write a short understanding statement of how you think the substance you may have been abusing has damaged your body's systems. What are the short- or long-term effects or what could they be.

_____
_____
_____
_____
_____
_____
_____
_____
_____
_____
_____
_____
_____
_____
_____

Pathway to an *Addiction Free* Lifestyle

PARTICIPANT EVALUATION FORM (MIDWAY)

What do you think of this group process?

_____
_____
_____
_____
_____
_____
_____
_____
_____
_____

Is this group process helping you? (circle one)   YES   NO

If this group process is guiding you towards your path of sobriety or "Wellbriety", please explain how.

_____
_____
_____
_____
_____
_____

_____

_____

_____

_____

_____

If this group process is not guiding you towards the path in which you seek, why do you think this process is not working?

_____

_____

_____

_____

_____

_____

_____

_____

_____

_____

After finishing this eight week course, would you like to attend mini workshops, in order to continue working on, or revising your Relapse Prevention Plan and your Life Plan? (circle one)

YES   NO

Please explain why.

_____

_____

Pathway to an *Addiction Free* Lifestyle

Comments and/or Suggestions:

WEEK FIVE

Learning Objectives

- ❖ 12-Step Process and Co-Dependency
- ❖ Time Management
- ❖ Self-Motivational Life Skills
- ❖ Insight and Remorse
- ❖ What is Insight and Remorse
- ❖ HIV/AIDS Health Care Issues

Pathway to an *Addiction Free* Lifestyle

GROUP DISCUSSION

WEEK FIVE

SESSION 1

12 STEP PROCESS AND CO-DEPENDENCY

This group discussion will help how and what the 12-Step process can do, and be brought into a strong 'Recovery and Social Wellness' (sober and well) life style. Each individual will be given information on how to identify and deal with co-dependency issues that can arise through treatment programs.

This will give each individual the power to live life on life's terms, knowing their strengths and weaknesses are all 'OK.' At the end of the session they will be able to start to apply these models to their daily lives, also with short- and long-term Life Plan goals in place.

Let us look how co-dependency behavior is discussed in the 'Sobriety and Wellness' Red Road to Recovery. White Bison, Inc.

Co-dependents are outwardly weak and insecure, seeking to lose themselves in others. They feel themselves to be dependent on another person and not really able to function on their own. People can be co-dependents to spouses, loved ones, friends, brothers, sisters, organizations, and other entities of all kinds.

Co-dependents tend to be the enablers in un-well situations like chemical dependency. Since they do not want to lose the other person, they make it very easy for the addict or alcoholic to keep using or drinking. We must remember that co-dependency is an emotional, psychological, behavioral, and spiritual condition that develops as a result of long-term exposure to a set of oppressive rules. Ask yourself, what type of oppressive rules did you live under?

Let us look at some of the characteristics of behavior patterns of co-dependent people:

1. **Relationship Addiction**: Co-dependents then treat love, work, or community relationships as an addiction.

2. **Lack of Boundaries**: Co-dependents do not know where they stop and others begin. They often take responsibility for others because they are not sure of whom they really are themselves.

3. **Impression Management**: Co-dependents tend to fake how they present themselves to others. They do not know how to have clear, straight interactions with others. Their 'outside' appearance is more important than their 'inside' feelings, intuition and stability.

4. **Caretaking**: Co-dependents must always be taking care of somebody or something.

5. **Physical Illness**: Co-dependents live under such relationships' stress that they often get sick.

6. **Control Issues**: Co-dependents are supreme controllers. They have to be on top of every situation. Being in control provides a sense of security.

7. **Distorted Feelings**: Co-dependents do not deal with feelings in a healthy way. They change their feelings to keep their image of themselves intact. For example: if something happens that brings up anger, it may be expressed as a smile, which is a distorted feeling/emotion.

8. **Thinking Disorders**: Co-dependents are often confused in their thinking, falling prey to either excessive or compulsive thinking patterns. For example: they can be obsessed by their work, leading to work-a-holism, etc. Or there can be such involvement with a social cause that other parts of a person's life becomes neglected.

9. **Manipulation**: Co-dependents place unrealistic demands on themselves and others. When these demands are not met, they place blame.

10. **Depression and Negativity**: Co-dependents can be chronically unhappy and see the dark, negative side of everything.

11. **Too Much Empathy**: Co-dependents feel for others and take on their problems in what is not quite 'true.' They are men/women who love too much.

12. **Inferiority/Low Self-Worth**: Co-dependents feel inferior and worthless as they interact and live in the world.

13. **Loss of Spirituality**: Co-dependents dishonesty not only leads to mistrust in ones' self and others, but also leads to a lack of faith in a Higher Power. Note: that is not a religion but a faith in something grander than themselves.

There are times in all our lives that we are in some form of co-dependency, and act as a codependent, but how we react to it or fall deeply into it is how we tend to live our lives. So, with an honest look into yourself answer the question: Where are you now?

_____

_____

_____

_____

_____

_____

_____

Pathway to an *Addiction Free* Lifestyle

GROUP DISCUSSION / PERSONNAL DEVELOPMENT

ASSIGNMENT

WEEK FIVE

SESSION 1

TIME MANAGEMENT

> *"I must govern the clock, not be governed by it."*
> Golda Meir

SUMMARY OF KEY CONCEPTS

In this session, we will discuss TIME MANAGEMENT. Also in this session, we will also use the Model For Control. We will also discuss two conditioning factors to look out for as we move toward taking more control of our time.

LEARNING OBJECTIVES:

By the end of this session, we should have an understanding of the following:

1. How to successfully take control of our time.

2. The conditioning factors to watch out for when taking control of our time.

3. A definition of inner peace.

CONCEPTS

SUCCESSFUL MANAGER OF TIME:

A successful manager of time is willing to do that which an unsuccessful manager of time is not willing to do.

WISDOM:

Wisdom is knowledge rightfully applied.

EINSTEIN'S DEFINITION OF TIME:

The occurrence of events in sequence one after the other.

MANAGEMENT:

The dictionary defines management as the art or act of controlling.

TIME MANAGEMENT:

Time management is the act of controlling events. To gain control of our lives, we must gain control of our time.

NATURAL LAW:

To gain control of our lives, we must gain control of our time.

CONTROL MODEL:

A MODEL FOR CONTROL

The more control you take, the more power you feel!

- What are some examples of events over which you have no control:

  _____

  _____

  _____

- What are some emotions you experience when you have no control:

  _____

  _____

  _____

- What are some examples of events over which you have total control:

  _____

  _____

  _____

- What are some emotions you experience when you have total control:

  _____

  _____

  _____

CONDITIONING FACTORS

As we move toward the control side, there are two conditioning factors you need to look out for:

Pathway to an *Addiction Free* Lifestyle

1. Events we can control but believe we cannot.

2. Events we cannot control but believe we can. INNER PEACE:

INNER PEACE:

Inner Peace is having serenity, balance, and harmony achieved through the appropriate control of events.

FIVE IMPORTANT STATEMENTS ABOUT GOALS

1. A goal is a planned for event.

2. When a goal is valued, it becomes a priority.

3. When goals are valued together, prioritizing is taking place.

4. Prioritizing is the process of determining the procedure of events.

5. The answers to the next two questions are very important to determining whether or not you become proactive in your life, or you stay reactive. Not just the answers to these questions, but what you do with the answers to these two questions will have a major impact on your future.

   A. What are the highest priorities in my life?

   _____
   _____
   _____

   B. Of these priorities, which do I value the most?

   _____
   _____
   _____

OBJECTIVE OF GOOD TIME MANAGEMENT

The objective of good time management is inner peace.

PLANNING:

Planning is predetermining a course of events.

COMMITMENT:

The act or an instance of committing. The state of being bound emotionally or intellectually to a course of action or to another person.

Rory C. Folsom & Steven D. Duby

WORKSHOP — MY CONTROL MODEL

What are the events that you have total control of in your life today, where you are right now:

- _____
- _____
- _____
- _____

What are the highest priorities in your life:

- _____
- _____
- _____
- _____

Of the priorities you have just listed, which three do you value most:

- _____
- _____

Write affirmations to bring the values that you have identified into your life.

1. _____
   _____

2. _____
   _____

3. _____
   _____

PERSONNAL DEVELOPMENT ASSIGNMENT

WEEK FIVE

TIME MANAGEMENT

Complete the Personal Development Assignment concerning Time Management. Let yourself reflect on how you managed your time during your period(s) of substance abuse. Now we must look into how we successfully manage time. We must learn to identify events that we have control over and the events we do not have control over. So for this assignment write down how you spent your day and what time you have control over and what time you have no control over.

Example: I woke up a 0530 and got ready for breakfast. After breakfast I studied my school work until 0930. Then I wanted to get an hour of jogging in, but it started to rain. Now what do I do?

1. Write out a time line of one(1) day of what you usually do.

_____

_____

_____

_____

_____

2. Write out what you would like your day to look like so you can get everything you want to accomplish done in a timely fashion.

_____

_____

_____

_____

Pathway to an *Addiction Free* Lifestyle
GROUP DISCUSSION

WEEK FIVE

SESSION 2

SELF-MOTIVATION LIFE SKILLS

This group will be given information and guidance on how self-motivation life skills and goal setting will help them from relapsing to the substance abuse life style. The lack of motivation is one of the biggest down-falls for an addict. If you can motivate someone to very short-term goals, like completing the assignments or just to do one thing every day, then move on up to longer-term goals, etc., you will provide the person with a method to see that they can accomplish these goals and this will lead to self-motivation. All of this builds one's self-confidence, and leads to their breaking their addiction. Next thing you know their emotional health starts to get stronger. Then more motivation sets in. Then long-term goals and 'Recovery and Social Wellness' life style comes into being and this is all part of the positive life cycle rather than the destructive substance abuse cycle they have been living.

Let us look at the Motivation Skills Check List within the Breaking Barriers Cognitive Reality Model by Gordon Graham.

Let us examine how we motivate ourselves and others

1. **Constructive Motivations**: Seeing the pay value or personal profitability which creates energy and excitement.

2. **Restrictive Motivation**: Seeing loss, based on fear, causes us to give up accountability for our actions and place the blame elsewhere.

3. **Inhibitive Motivation**: Is where we feel 'I can't, or else....'

Pathway to an *Addiction Free* Lifestyle

GROUP DISCUSSION / PERSONNAL DEVELOPMENT

ASSIGNMENT

WEEK FIVE

SESSION 2

MOTIVATIONAL CHECKLIST

> *"The great thing in this world is not so much where we are, but in what direction we are moving."*
> Oliver Wendell Holmes

SUMMARY OF KEY CONCEPTS

This session examines how we motivate ourselves and others. Constructive Motivation, seeing the pay value or personal profitability, creates energy and excitement. Restrictive Motivation, seeing the loss, based on fear, causes us to give up accountability for our actions and place the blame elsewhere. Inhibitive Motivation is where we feel "I can't, or else ..."

LEARNING OBJECTIVES:

By the end of this session, we should have an understanding of the following:

1. What happens when we constructively motivate ourselves and others?

2. What happens when we restrictively motivate ourselves and others?

3. Ways in which we use inhibitive motivation to give up accountability in our lives?

CONCEPTS

CONSTRUCTIVE MOTIVATION:

Seeing the pay value or personal profitability. Wanting to, choosing to. Looking at the options and accepting accountability.

RESTRICTIVE MOTIVATION:

Based on fear. Seeing the loss. Giving up accountability and fixing the blame for failure somewhere outside ourselves.

INHIBITIVE MOTIVATION:

Inhibitive motivation is a form of restrictive motivation. It is when we can't, "or else" something bad will happen.

CONSTRUCTIVE AND RESTRICTIVE MOTIVATION

CONSTRUCTIVE	RESTRICTIVE
Picture the win	*Picture the loss*
See the possibilities	*Creatively avoid*
Has energy	*Lack energy*
Creative	*Lack creativity*

Listed above are all the differences between "**Possibility Thinkers**," who constructively motivate themselves, and "**Impossibility Thinkers**," who restrictively motivate themselves.

The key to all motivation is to see the personal pay value of what we are doing. It is very important that we recognize how we talk to ourselves, whether from the constructive side or the restrictive side. It's clearer that "I want to" rather than "I have to" is far the best way to motivate ourselves to reach the goals we set.

In order to constructively motivate change, it's important to ask ourselves, "Why do I do this? What will it do for me and others who are important to me?"

We need to develop the habit of making our own choices ... looking at all of the options and then making our own choices. Our choices may not always be great, but there are always choices, and if we don't make our own, someone else will make them for us.

When we restrictively motivate ourselves, we are saying we don't have any control of our lives. "It's not my fault," means we are letting others control our actions. We want to "fix the blame fast" for what happens to us in our lives.

"If it's to be, it's up to me," means we are looking at where we are today, where we want to be, and then WE are choosing what we want to do to get there.

LOOKING AT MOTIVATION

Look at just a few of the RUTS that you have experienced in your life. How would/does motivation fit in? Are you constructively or restrictively motivating yourself to change these areas of your life?

RUT: _____

How can you constructively motivate yourself to overcome this issue?

_____

_____

What is the pay value in changing this issue?

_____

_____

RUT: _____

How can you constructively motivate yourself to overcome this issue?

_____

_____

What is the pay value in changing this issue?

_____

_____

RUT: _____

How can you constructively motivate yourself to overcome this issue?

_____

_____

What is the pay value in changing this issue?

Pathway to an *Addiction Free* Lifestyle
GROUP DISCUSSION

WEEK FIVE

SESSION 3

INSIGHT, REMORSE AND INSIGHT INTO YOUR SUBSTANCE ABUSE

This group session will deal directly with what is Insight & Remorse. The reason why the individuals need to know what Insight is: it is to allow them to truly understand their addiction in every respect, and how to take ownership of their individual recovery.

Remorse, or how can or what would anyone want to change regarding their past actions. Also, if they cannot understand or comprehend the hurt and pain they have caused directly or indirectly during their path of substance abuse this needs to be dealt with as part of their Insight.

Then, the Personal Development Assignment will be discussed from page H-41.

Complete the assignment by reading the Handout(s) and write a one (1) page review of your Insight into your substance abuse. Then describe by name someone you have hurt by your direct actions.

Now the Personal Development Assignment will be discussed concerning the treatments for the different viruses that are contracted via substance abuse, such as HIV/AIDS on H-41.

Pathway to an *Addiction Free* Lifestyle

GROUP DISCUSSION

WEEK FIVE

SESSION 3

Important

Define Remorse and Responsibility. Explain the difference between the two.

1. Remorse: Feeling of Sorrow for a choice or decision made.

2. Responsibility: The conscious choice to actively seek out those character flaws inside of you that made / makes it "Ok" for you to commit criminal acts.

3. True remorse drives you to responsibility.

QUESTIONS TO ASK YOURSELF

1. Who was your victim? Who is/was he/she as a person?

   _____
   _____
   _____

2. What was going on in your life a week before your crime or episode? What about three days before?

   _____
   _____
   _____

3. What was your emotional state those three days before your crime or episode? Were you using drugs or alcohol?

4. If you were using, why?

5. What was your emotional state the day of your crime or episode?

6. After you did what you did, what was your first reaction? Why?

7. What events led up to your crime or episode? Make a timeline and map out key points that led you to commit the act. What could you/should you have done differently at each point?

Pathway to an *Addiction Free* Lifestyle
PERSONAL DEVELOPMENT

ASSIGNMENT

WEEK FIVE

INSIGHT AND REMORSE

Complete the Personal Development Assignment by reading the Handout(s) and write a one (1) page review of your Insight into your substance abuse. Then describe by name someone you have hurt by your direct actions.

HIV/AIDS HEALTH CARE ISSUES

In this Personal Development Assignment the group will be given HIV/AIDS Health Care Services Division Educational Services Unit handout starting on H-41 to be read and complete the ten (10) questions quiz.

_____
_____
_____
_____
_____
_____
_____
_____
_____
_____
_____
_____
_____

WEEK SIX

Learning Objective

- ❖ Stress: Introduction to Creative Visualization
- ❖ Daily Relaxation Program
- ❖ Type 'A' Behavior Pattern Forgiveness & Spiritual Health Dimension
- ❖ Understanding Type 'A' Behavior Patterns
- ❖ Traumatic Events and Post-Traumatic Stress Disorder (PTSD)
- ❖ Family of Origin and Your Role

GROUP DISCUSSION

WEEK SIX

SESSION 1

STRESS: INTRODUCTION TO CREATIVE VISUALIZATION

During this group discussion we will identify and introduce to the individuals to what is stress and how to deal with it without turning to substance abuse. Methods of stress reduction such as: Creative Visualization, Meditation, Breathing Through your Abdomen, etc. will be introduced to the group.

There are several different aspects of stress and you also must keep in mind that all stress in not bad stress. But for this group discussion, we are looking at the negative side of stress that leads us to substance abuse because we cannot handle it with the tools we used to have. Stress is defined as:

- A. Mental or emotional tension or strain characterized by feelings of anxiety, fear, etc.

- B. A factor or combination of factors that cause tension or strain, as an urgent need to or perceived threat.

- C. Psychological: A condition typically characterized by symptoms of mental and physical tension or strain, as depression or hypertension that can result from a reaction to a situation in which a person feels threatened, pressured, etc.

Since everyone is different, each person will experience stress and stress relief uniquely. We must recognize these differences within ourselves. So we want you all to find that 'internal harmony,' to heal the emotional and physical upsets, to increase body awareness, thus leading to stress reduction and enhanced relaxation. If we can just reduce some of our daily stress this just might be enough to keep us from feeling helpless or hopeless. This reduction will reduce the chance for us to return to substance abuse, which we use to relieve those stress perceptions.

Let us look at some very simple ways to reduce stress by relaxation.

1. One very simple technique is, as you wake up in the morning do a daily review and visualize where and when you are going to be doing your most work and projects. What is it going to entail to complete this day. Just close your eyes and do some very deep and easy belly breathing and with your mind's eye walk through the possible day. The areas that you may feel yourself getting tense, for example: I have a test in College Math at 2:00 PM but I have to have a meeting with my work supervisor over a big work load for today. Think over that a couple of times and do it over and over. While you are breathing and visualizing your day, think of taking the meeting then take the test while you are controlling your breathing. Then stop thinking about it

and visualize some beautiful sunset or lake. Then open your eyes. Now you have done the meeting several times in your mind and you have taken the test several times in your mind, you will be ready and not stressed out.

2. A second way is to meditate twice a day just by sitting very quietly with your back straight, First talk to yourself in a very soft manner to let yourself know what you want to do. Relax: then while you take three (3) deep belly breaths then start to focus on the bottom of your feet and visualize the muscles unwinding and move up your body, to your ankles, calves, legs, thighs, stomach, chest, shoulder, down each arm, up through the neck, you face, then let the energy just pass right out of the top of your head. Then as you're realizing think about a beautiful light of warm energy coming down from above and entering through the top of your head and following the same path back down through your body until it connect you to the earth. Carry that energy with you all day and at the end of the day release it the same way. This will let any stored up negative energy giving you a restful night sleep.

3. Listening to very soft music (flute or jazz) and just reviewing the day with your eyes closed and letting those things that may have given you tension allow yourself to let them go and not have any power over you. Do not let anyone or thing have power over your thought. Once we lose that control we will live a life filled with stress. Then health problems will arrive. Disease comes from distress which comes from unease/disease. We must always remember that the only person that can get you angry, sad, mad, or stressed out is YOU!!! Everyone has the power to not allow ANY event to control your feelings. NO ONE can make you hurt yourself by substance abuse except you.

Now let us do a five (5) minute visualization exercise.

Pathway to an *Addiction Free* Lifestyle

PERSONAL DEVELOPMENT ASSIGNMENT

WEEK SIX

SESSION 1

STRESS MANAGEMENT EXERCISES

MINIMIZING THE EFFECTS OF STRESS

Sometimes stressful situations persist despite our best efforts to resolve them. Knowing that chronic stress can jeopardize your health, what can you do to minimize the adverse impact of stress on your physical well-being? Here are four practical suggestions.

Suggestion 1: *Avoid or Minimize the Use of Stimulates*

In dealing with stressful situations, people often turn to stimulants to help keep them going, such as coffee or caffeinated energy drinks. If you know someone who smokes you have probably observed that most smokers react to stress by increasing their smoking. The problem is that common stimulants like caffeine and nicotine actually work against you in coping with stress. They increase the psychological effects of stress by raising heart rate and blood pressure. In effect, users of stimulant drugs are already primed to respond with greater reactivity, exaggerating the psychological consequences of stress.

The best advice? Avoid stimulant drugs altogether. If that is not possible, make a conscious effort to monitor your use of stimulants, especially when you are under stress. You will find it easier to deal with stressors when your nervous system is not already in high gear because of caffeine, nicotine, or other stimulants. Minimizing your use of stimulants will also make it easier for you to implement the next suggestion.

Suggestion 2: *Exercise Regularly*

Numerous studies all point to the same conclusion: Regular exercise, particularly aerobic exercise like walking, swimming, or running, is one of the best ways to reduce the impact of stress. The key word here is *regular*. Try walking briskly for 20 minutes, four or five times a week. It will improve your physical health and help you cope with stress. In fact, just about any kind Of physical exercise helps buffer the negative effects of stress.

(Rapidly pushing the channel up/down buttons on your television doesn't count)

Compared to sofa slugs, physically fit people are less physiologically reactive to stressors and produce lower levels of stress hormones. Psychologically, regular exercises reduces anxiety and depressed feelings and increases self-confidence and self-esteem.

Suggestion 3: *Get Enough Sleep*

With the ongoing push to get more and more done, people often stretch their days by shortchanging themselves on sleep. But sleep deprivation just adds to your feelings of stress. "Without sufficient sleep it is more difficult to concentrate, make careful decisions, and follow instructions," explains researcher Mark Rosekind (2003). You are more likely to make mistakes or errors, and are more prone to being impatient and lethargic. And, your attention, memory and reaction time are all adversely affected.

The stress-sleep connection also has the potential to become a vicious cycle. School, work, and family related pressures contribute to reduced or disturbed sleep, leaving you less than adequately rested and making efforts to deal with the situation all the more taxing and distressful. And inadequate sleep, even for just a few nights, takes a physical toll on the body, leaving us more prone to health problems.

<u>Suggestion 4</u>: *Practice a Relaxation Technique*

You can significantly reduce stress-related symptoms by regularly using any one of a variety of relaxation techniques. Meditation is one effective stress reduction strategy. There are many different meditation techniques, but they all involve focusing mental attention, heightening awareness, and quieting internal chatter. Most meditation techniques are practiced while sitting quietly, but others involve movement, such as yoga and walking meditation. Many studies have demonstrated the physical and psychological benefits of meditation. More specifically, meditation has been shown to reduce both the psychological and the physiological effects of stress.

One form of meditation that has been receiving a great deal of attention in psychology is called *mindfulness meditation*. Mindfulness techniques were developed as a Buddhist practice more than two thousand years ago, but modern psychologists and other health practioners have adapted these practices for use in a secular context.

Definitions of mindfulness are as varied as the practices associated with it. It is important to note, also, that strictly speaking, mindfulness refers to an approach to everyday life as well as a formal meditation technique. However, for our purposes, **Mindfulness Meditation** can be defined as a technique in which practitioners focus awareness on present experience with acceptance.

Advocates of mindfulness practice believe that most psychological distress is caused by a person's reactions to events and circumstances, their emotions, thoughts, and judgments. As psychologist Mark Williams points out, "We are always explaining the world to ourselves, and we react emotionally to these explanations rather than to the facts. Thoughts are not facts." Mindfulness practice is a way to correct that habitual perspective, clearing and calming the mind in the process. David Ludwig and Jon Kabat-Zinn (2008) explain:

> *Mindfulness can be considered a universal human capacity proposed to foster clear thinking and open-heartedness. As such, this form of meditation requires no particular religious or cultural believe system. The goal of mindfulness is to maintain awareness moment by moment, disengaging oneself from strong*

Pathway to an *Addiction Free* Lifestyle

attachments to beliefs, thoughts, or emotions, thereby developing a greater sense of emotional balance and well-being.

In other words, mindfulness meditation involves paying attention to your ongoing mental experience in a nonjudgmental, nonreactive manner.

Pathway to an *Addiction Free* Lifestyle
PERSONAL DEVELOPMENT ASSIGNMENT

WEEK SIX

SESSION 1

DAILY RELAXATION PROGRAM

To complete this Personal Development Assignment look at what causes your stress and put into effect a relaxation program into your daily routine. Then start to list it in your Life Plan.

For Example: Knowing that it may take some time to get the right employment to pay your bills instead of stressing yourself out every week, set up a one (1) hour time of self-reflection and exercise.

On the previous pages, there is a Stress Management Exercises to practice.

Write down five (5) different actions that you can do to relieve stress on a daily basis to help you on your relapse prevention plan.

_____
_____
_____
_____
_____
_____
_____
_____
_____
_____
_____
_____
_____

Pathway to an *Addiction Free* Lifestyle

GROUP DISCUSSION

WEEK SIX

SESSION 2

TYPE 'A' BEHAVIOR PATTERNS

This group discussion will explore how the 'Type A' behavior pattern associates with substance abuse. This pattern is expressed by the projection of three (3) specific behavior traits that are obvious in everyday life. It is exhibited by:

1. An exaggerated sense of time urgency, often trying to do more and more in less and less time.

2. A general sense of hostility, frequently displaying anger and irritation.

3. Intense ambition and competitiveness.

'Type A's tend to react more intensely to a stressor then other people do. As a result they experience greater increases in blood pressure, heart rate, and the production of stress related hormones.

Hostile attitudes and behaviors also tend to create more stress in one's everyday life: in effect they experience more frequent and more severe emotional actions leading to negative life events and more daily hassles than other individuals.

These conditions leave those individuals to seek ways to relieve this condition and since they can not go on vacation every day, they seek instant ways such as substance abuse which leads to greater problems as we all know full well.

With the 'Type A' behavior patterns, let us take a look at Spirituality. The spiritual dimension or renewing of the spiritual dimension provides leadership to your life. The spiritual dimension is your core, your center, your commitment to your value system. (Covey, 1989)

1. Hockenbury & Hockenbury, title, Discovering Psychology, 4th Ed. 2007

Pathway to an Addiction Free Lifestyle

GROUP DISCUSSION

WEEK SIX

SESSION 2

TYPE "A" BEHAVIOR PATTERNS

The concept of Type "A" behavior originated about 30 years ago, when two cardiologists, Meyer Friedman and Ray Rosenman, noticed that many of their patients shared certain traits. The original formulation of the Type "A" behavior pattern included a cluster of three characteristics:

1. An exaggerated sense of time urgency, often trying to do more and more in less and less time.

2. A general sense of hostility, frequently displaying anger and irritation.

3. Intense ambition and competitiveness.

Although early results linking the Type "A" behavior pattern to heart disease were impressive, studies soon began to appear in which Type "A" behavior did not reliably predict the development of heart disease, but did show signs of hyper tension.

Feeling a sense of time urgency and being competitive or achievement oriented did not seem to be associated with the development of heart disease. Instead, the critical component that emerged as the strongest predictor of cardiac disease was hostility. **Hostility** *refers to the tendency to feel anger, annoyance, resentment, and contempt, and to hold cynical and negative beliefs about human nature in general.* Hostile people are also prone to believing that the disagreeable behavior of others is intentionally directed against them. Thus, hostile people tend to be **suspicious, mistrustful, cynical, and pessimistic.** (Sound Familiar?)

Hostile people are much more likely than other people to develop heart disease, even when other risk factors are taken into account. In one study that covered a 25-year span, hostile men were five times as likely to develop heart disease and nearly seven times as likely to die as non-hostile men. As we look at this Type "A" behavior pattern one must understand that 90% of incarcerated males have a Type "A" personality and tend to react more intensely to a stressor than other people do. And the fabrication of these actions increases our blood pressure, heart rate, and the production of stress-related hormones. Because of our attitudes and behavior, hostile men and women also tend to create more stress in our own lives.

Pathway to an *Addiction Free* Lifestyle

GROUP DISCUSSION

WEEK SIX

SESSION 2

TYPE "A" BEHAVIOR PATTERNS

We experience more frequent, and more severe, negative life events and daily hassles than other people. As a Type "A" personality, we must look at how we are handling each situation we get ourselves into. Since we make ourselves even more stressed out due to this behavior pattern, we tend to look for ways to escape through destructive actions such as drugs, alcohol and different violent pathways.

Reflect back on your life, and really look at how each one of us handled different situations in our lives, and how much we each contributed to making the problem bigger than it needed to be, just because of our perceptions. How many times did we make a small problem into a big one due to having a hostile attitude? We must honestly look at ourselves in a way that helps us work on reducing the stressful factors in our daily lives that can and will lead us back to the same destructive behavior and/or addictions that has all of us sitting here today, seeking

"FORGIVENESS", "REDEMPTION",

AND

"A PATHWAY TO FREEDOM"

Pathway to an *Addiction Free* Lifestyle

PERSONAL DEVELOPMENT ASSIGNMENT

WEEK SIX

SESSION 2

UNDERSTANDING TYPE 'A' BEHAVIOR PATTERNS

This Personal Development Assignment is for the understanding of the 'Type A' behavior patterns and how your pattern has caused harm and how we obtain forgiveness to all involved. These include but are not limited to Victim(s), Family, Community, and Self.

In a 12-Step process/program like AA/NA the steps are the same as in Step Eight where you are willing to make a list of those you have harmed and are willing to make amends to. The Ninth Step- is that you make amends to those people whenever you can, except when to do so would harm them more.

Forgiveness starts to mend the wreckage that we have done by our actions during our substance abuse. First, you truly acknowledge in a good way that we have hurt people while we were drinking or drugging even if we do not remember it. This has to be by your own doing. No one can make you forgive. We must come to an understanding that we are connected to all things. When we accept that truth instead of the comfort of denial, we become willing to look at our part in the creation of harm.

If we truly want to make up for the hurts we have caused, then we must be completely honest in the forgiveness process and be present in the amends we will do with each other. We also must remember that we may forgive others but they do not have to forgive us. But once you have made the effort and are living in the right balance life style, it is all you can do, it is all of what you have control of. There is always the idea that we have told people the words and apologized or say "I am sorry,' but then a day, a week, or a month later we do the same thing all over again. Others may not want to hear the words but they may want you to show them (over time) that you have changed, or they may even totally ignore your amends.

For this Personal Development Assignment, on a separate piece of paper list the people you have harmed and think of one way to not only forgive yourself but forgive one other person.

Pathway to an *Addiction Free* Lifestyle

Pathway to an *Addiction Free* Lifestyle

GROUP DISCUSSION

WEEK SIX

SESSION 3

TRAUMATIC EVENTS AND POST-TRAUMATIC STRESS DISORDER (PTSD)

This group discussion will deal with the different aspects of traumatic events in each individual's life which may have caused a condition of Post-Traumatic Stress Disorder (PTSD). PTSD causes many emotional effects that the individual many not know they are acting the way they are, and until they do the personal inventory this individual will be at a loss. Discuss the individual's family of origin and their role in the family and what it is suppose to be. There will be an open discussion as what we are: as a benefit or the creator of pain and loss.

Let us take a look at how PTSD is defined within The DSM-IV-TR § 309.81: New DSM-V

- A. The person has been exposed to a traumatic event in which both of the following were present:

  - (1) the person experienced, witnessed, or was confronted with an event or events that involved actual or threatened death or serious injury, or a threat to the physical integrity of self or others.

  - (2) the person's response involved intense fear, helplessness, or horror. NOTE: In children, this may be expressed instead by disorganized or agitated behavior.

- B. The traumatic event is persistently re-experienced in one (or more) of the following ways:

  - (1) recurrent and intrusive distressing recollections of the event, including images, thoughts, or perceptions

  - (2) recurrent distressing dreams of the event

  - (3) acting or feeling as if the traumatic event were recurring (includes a sense of reliving the experience, illusions, hallucinations, and dissociative flashback episodes, including those that occur on awakening or when intoxicated)

  - (4) intense psychological distress at exposure to internal or external cues that symbolize or resemble an aspect of the traumatic event

  - (5) physiological reactivity on exposure to internal or external cues that symbolize or resemble an aspect of the traumatic event

C. Persistent avoidance of stimuli associated with their trauma and numbing of general responsiveness (not present before the trauma), as indicated by three (or more) of the following:

    (1) efforts to avoid thought, feelings, or conversations associated with the events to trauma

    (2) efforts to avoid activities, place, or people that arouse recollections of the trauma

    (3) inability to recall an important aspect of the trauma

    (4) markedly diminished interest or participation in significant activities

    (5) feeling of detachment or estrangement from others

    (6) restricted range of affect (e.g., unable to have loving feelings)

    (7) sense of a foreshortened future (e.g., does not expect to have a career, marriage, children, or a normal life span)

D. Persistent symptoms of increased arousal (not present before the trauma), as indicated by two (or more) of the following:

    (1) difficulty falling or staying asleep

    (2) irritability or outburst of anger

    (3) difficulty concentrating

    (4) hyper vigilance

    (5) exaggerated startle response

E. Duration of the disturbance (symptoms in criteria B.C. and D.) is more than one (1) month.

F. The disturbance causes clinically significant distress or impairment in social, occupational, or other important areas of functioning.

    ACUTE: If duration of symptoms is less than three (3) months.

    CHRONIC: If duration of symptoms is three (3) months or more.

So during your personal inventory we must look honestly at what has or may have happened in our lives that could be considered as a traumatic event that could lead us into substance abuse.

Here is one major way that can help you look into your past: 'Family of Origin.' The different family members and their roles within the respective families of origin, i.e.; father role, son role, etc. By examining the family of origin we will be encouraged to face the realities of our childhood, and in turn comparing our own place in our children's family of origin. We will also explore the dynamics of the relationships between a man role and a women role as it related to the beginning of a family. The importance of this relationship is the determinant in the function ability of the family unit and some key points in creating a successful picture of your past and the effects that lead you here today.

_____
_____
_____
_____
_____
_____
_____
_____
_____
_____
_____
_____
_____
_____
_____
_____
_____
_____
_____
_____
_____
_____
_____
_____

Pathway to an Addiction Free Lifestyle

Pathway to an *Addiction Free* Lifestyle

PERSONAL DEVELOPMENT ASSIGNMENT

WEEK SIX

FAMILIY OF ORIGIN AND YOUR ROLE

For this Personal Development Assignment, on the lines below, the group must complete the 'Family of Origin' genogram on page 137, 139 and write a short story of how, if any, traumatic event(s) may have caused emotional distress that if not dealt with in a proper manner could lead you back to substance abuse.

_____

_____

_____

_____

_____

_____

_____

_____

_____

_____

_____

_____

_____

_____

Pathway to an *Addiction Free* Lifestyle

Pathway to an *Addiction Free* Lifestyle

GROUP DISCUSSION / PERSONNAL DEVELOPMENT ASSIGNMENT

WEEK SIX

SESSION 3

<u>GENEALOGY</u>

THE GENOGRAM

Since Bowen believed multigenerational patterns and influences are crucial determinants of nuclear family functioning, he developed a graphic way of investigating the genesis of the presenting problem by diagramming the family over at least three generations. To aid in the process and to keep the record in pictorial form in front of him he constructed a family genogram in which each partner's family background is laid out. Worked out with the family during early sessions, it provides a useful tool for allowing therapist and family members alike to examine the ebb and flow of the family's emotional process in their intergenerational context. Each individual's family(s) biological, kinship, and psychosocial makeup can be gleaned from pursuing this visual graph (Roberto, 1992).

Figure 1.1 on page 137, offers a partial set of commonly used genogram symbols. Together, the symbols provide a visual picture of a tree: who the members are, what their names are, age, sibling positions, marital status, divorces, adoptions, co-dependent, chemical or alcohol dependent, and so on, typically extending back at least three generations for both partners. When relevant, additional items of information such as religious affiliation, work histories, ethnic origins, geographic locations, socioeconomic status, noteworthy health issues, and perhaps significant life events may be included. More than providing a concise pictorial depiction of the nuclear family, the genogram may suggest certain emotional patterns in each partner's family of origin, thus providing data for assessing each spouse's degree of fusion to extended families and to one another.

Genograms often give families their first inkling of intergenerational family relationship patterns. You will be able to note how many hypothesis springs from genograms, to be explored with the family subsequently. Fusion-differentiation issues in the family of origin, the nuclear family emotional system, emotional cutoffs by the parents, sibling positions, and many other concepts appear relevant to presenting symptoms. When evaluation interview data are put into schematic form in a family genogram, therapist and family together are better able to comprehend the underlying emotional processes, connecting generations. In a sense, the family genogram is never completed, as information uncovered during the course of therapy sheds new light on basic patterns of emotional reactivity in both the nuclear and extended families. Major turning points for the family (such as the unexpected death of a key family member) may mark the start of a series of family problems that may reverberate across generations (Papero, 1990). Genograms are thus a relatively emotion-free way of collecting information that makes sense of the family and connects them to the therapeutic process.

Pathway to an *Addiction Free* Lifestyle

GROUP DISCUSSION / PERSONNAL DEVELOPMENT ASSIGNMENT

WEEK SIX

SESSION 3

<u>GENEALOGY</u>

The following is a key to building your own genogram.

NOTE: The age of each individual is placed inside of the symbol and the name is placed above, below or even next to symbol. For married couples, you place the year in which they were married on the line adjoining the two, as well as separation or divorce (m = married, d = divorced, s = separated). Examples: m 78 (married in 1978), s 85 — d 87 (separated in 1985 and divorced in 1987).

Figure 1.1

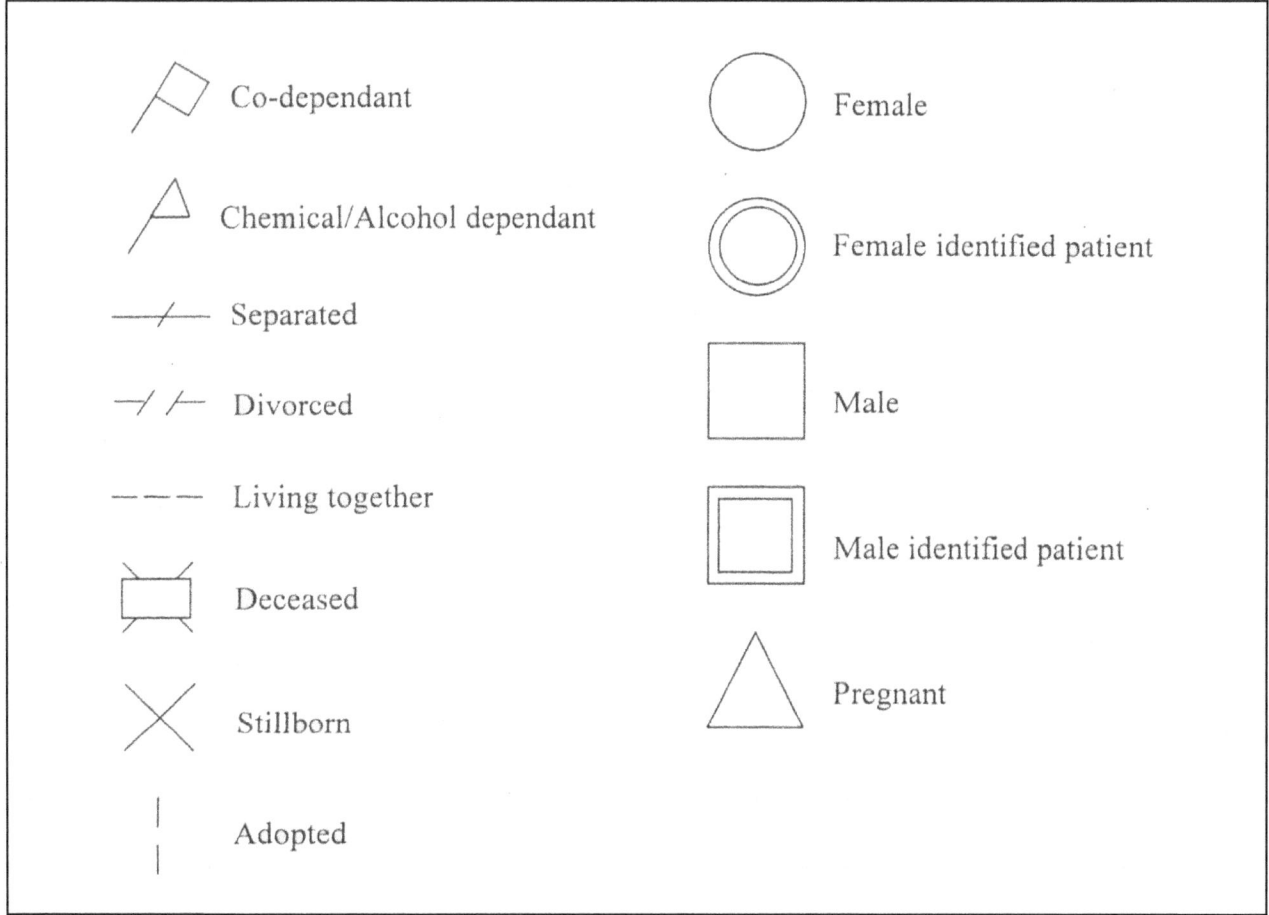

Pathway to an *Addiction Free* Lifestyle

GROUP DISCUSSION/PERSONNAL DEVELOPMENT ASSIGNMENT

WEEK SIX

GENEALOGY

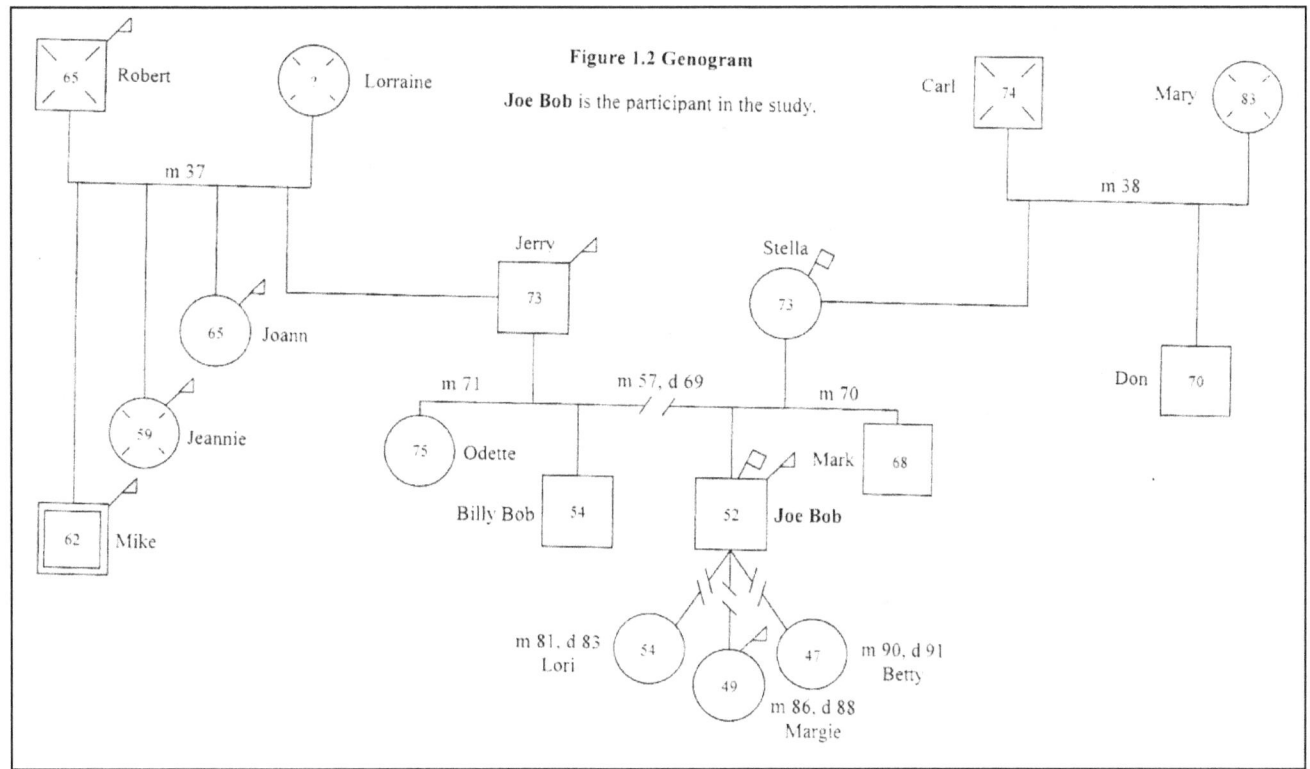

Figure 1.2 Genogram

WEEK SEVEN

Learning Objective

- ❖ Compared Life Styles Mind Mapping
- ❖ Social Factors and The Life Cycle
- ❖ Gender Roles and Gender Ideology
- ❖ Botulism, Risk Behavior and Staph. / MRSA
- ❖ Family Dynamics in Drug Abuse
- ❖ Family Dynamics/How to Improve and Stop the Abuse Cycle

Pathway to an *Addiction Free* Lifestyle

GROUP DISCUSSION

WEEK SEVEN

SESSION I

MIND MAPPING: COMPARED LIFESTYLES

This group discussion and lesson plan will allow each individual to be able to focus on the life they have lead with substance abuse verses a life they could look at without substance abuse.

To make a 'Mind Map,' draw a circle in the center of a piece of paper, just like the handout F-1. Inside the circle write 'Powerless' over whatever has been abused. Now begin a brainstorming session with yourself. Think about everything that hurt you or the losses that have meaning to you. Each time you think of something write it down in a few words on one of the branches leading from the 'Mind Map.' Each time you think of something that goes deeper into your thoughts write it down. Always start on the left side of your 'Mind Map'. After you have completed the left side of your 'Mind Map,' now look at the right side of the map and start to vision what your life would be like if you did not have a substance abuse problem. For every title you put into the circle repeat the process starting with you then work you way out to Relationships; Jobs; Family Visions; Life Plan; Community.

By the time you have completed both sides of this lesson the individual should have a very clear understanding of what their life looked like with substance abuse and what it is going to look like without the substance abuse. This understanding will give them the power to change their path by self-awareness and also give it a direction to change.

Pathway to an *Addiction Free* Lifestyle

Pathway to an *Addiction Free* Lifestyle

PERSONAL DEVELOPMENT ASSIGNMENT

WEEK SEVEN

SESSION 1

SOCIAL FACTORS, THE LIFE CYCLE AND MIND MAPPING

This Personal Development Assignment session will explore the social class lifestyles and cultural backgrounds that are interlinked and play a vital role in the way a family proceeds in its life cycle.

We explore the significant differences in traditions, rituals, and ceremonies that mark life cycle transitions. We examine the degrees of ethnic identification, social class, religion, politics, geography, and the severity of perceived or real discrimination as they relate to acculturation and anti-social behavioral patterns.

With all this in mind, take some time to write down, on a separate piece of paper, a page how you feel your culture and family background, and society, had what type of impact on your substance abuse. Do this, as well as the completion of the 'Mind Mapping' exercise.

_____

_____

_____

_____

_____

_____

_____

_____

_____

_____

_____

_____

Pathway to an *Addiction Free* Lifestyle

GROUP DISCUSSION

WEEK SEVEN

SESSION 2

GENDER ROLES AND GENDER IDEOLOGY

This group discussion will focus on Gender Roles and Gender Ideology. Keeping in mind that gender shapes our individual identity and expectations, our role and status within our family, all the while having the real and perceived life choices that are open to us. This session will examine male and female indoctrination into different socially based gender roles and behavior. While biology dictates the role in gender differences, we will examine the cognitive factors, value systems, Reality characteristics, along with problem solving techniques dealing with attitude towards sexuality, etc.

(Goldenberg & Goldenberg, 2008)

Society's perception of traditional male dominance in everyday life has changed dramatically over the recent decades. We will also examine the collision of the old cultural norms, now confronted with the new ideas and beliefs concerning this issue. Discussion on how these new gender roles affect substance abuse.

Pathway to an *Addiction Free* Lifestyle

PERSONAL DEVELOPMENT ASSIGNMENT

WEEK SEVEN

BOTULISM AND STAPH. / MRSA

This Personal Development Assignment is to read the IPEP handout H-81 dealing with botulism, staph. / MRSA infections that can and will happen during certain substance abuse like pruno cooking, drug use, dirty spoons/needles, water, etc. Read material and be prepared to discuss it at the next group meeting.

_____

_____

_____

_____

_____

_____

_____

_____

_____

_____

_____

_____

Pathway to an *Addiction Free* Lifestyle

Pathway to an *Addiction Free* Lifestyle

GROUP DISCUSSION

WEEK SEVEN

SESSION 3

FAMILY DYNAMICS IN DRUG ABUSE AND

THE FIVE STAGES OF REACTION

This group discussion will focus on the family dynamics in a substance abuse life style.

With this session let us look at how the family has coped with having a substance abuser as a family member in an effort to understand the origins of the abuse cycles.

With this knowledge it will help maximize the chances of a successful recovery and maintenance. We will learn the pattern of family reactions to the conditions of substance abuse. These reactions are very similar with the stages of grief, which are DENIAL, ANGER, BARGAINING, FEELING, and finally ACCEPTANCE. This is a very important part of recovery for not only the substance abuser but for the family as well.

Denial: After the initial shock of living a life out of control by substance abuse, denial is a normal first reaction. During the stage of denial, the attitudes of an addict's family and friends are critical in the aspect of intervention. These attitudes may very well be the difference between a path of addiction and a path to recovery for the affected person.

Anger: It is important that individuals recognize the need for those who are getting clean and sober to express their anger, whether they direct it towards their family, friends, belief system or even counselors. If this displaced anger is taken personally, any meaningful dialog with the substance abuser will be cut off.

Bargaining: Most substance abusers use this stage often. Bargaining typically involves change in behavior or a specific promise in exchange for more time to change. (i.e. "God, if you get me out of this I will change" or "I'll never drink again if you'll just let me live.")

Feeling: Recovering addicts look at their past actions and have many different feelings. Just as it had been important to allow yourself to fully vent your anger, it is important to express your sadness, and/or any other built-up emotions which may block the recovery process.

Acceptance: Acceptance of addiction can be reached if you work through the many conflicts and feelings that substance abuse brings. You are in this stage when you have worked through the physical symptoms and the psychological struggle is over. Be prepared that not all recovering addicts have a beautiful, blissful, insightful, forgiving experience; many are and will be downright angry and resentful.

Pathway to an *Addiction Free* Lifestyle
PERSONAL DEVELOPMENT ASSIGNMENT

WEEK SEVEN

FIVE STAGES OF REACTION

This personal Development Assignment is to write a short statement on the lines below about how your family and you dealt with those five (5) stages of reactions to your substance abuse and the conditions that were caused by your abuse.

DENIAL:

_____
_____
_____
_____

ANGER:

_____
_____
_____
_____

BARGAINING:

_____
_____
_____
_____

FEELING:

_____
_____
_____
_____

ACCEPTANCE:

WEEK EIGHT

Learning Objectives

- ❖ Survival Roles and Copying Mechanisms
- ❖ Complete your Life Plan Outline
- ❖ Relapse Prevention
- ❖ Program Overview and Counselor Assignment
- ❖ Group Graduation

Pathway to an *Addiction Free* Lifestyle

GROUP DISCUSSION

WEEK EIGHT

SESSION 1

SURVIVAL ROLES and COPING MECHANISMS

This group discussion will cover several areas of survival roles and coping mechanisms. These areas include how to bring the self-awareness, anger management, and family roles into the 'Recovery and Social Wellness' techniques. These new life skills can be applied to your daily Life Plan.

We will examine the interpersonal problems associated with the family unit as it relates to a member begin dependent. The group will discuss the roles which help the family to eventually reconstruct a functional family unit. We will discuss the five (5) primary family survival roles that are used as coping, mechanisms.

1. Chief Enabler
2. Family Hero
3. Family Scapegoat
4. The Lost Child
5. Family Mascot

The discussion will emphasize the need for the entire family to re-establish communication; to work through old resentments; to develop trust and; to strive to engage in a comfortable and rewarding relationship. A substance abuse free family is more than a family without drugs/alcohol in their lives. It is a family completely changed in their way of thinking, acting, communicating which all is leading into a totally different life style from which they have been living in.

Another coping skill that you have learned is stress management. One very good way is to review your daily use of the 12-Step method of Step Ten (10). We continue to think about our strengths and weaknesses and when we are wrong we say so. This does not mean just if we are wrong to other people, it also means if we have wronged ourselves. Evaluate your day not only with yourself, but with someone you trust, like your wife, brother, child, sister, friend, or sponsor.

Anger! Let us remind ourselves to take just a few seconds before any words come out of our mouth. Ask yourself: Why do I feel this way about what just was said or was done? After we become aware of our personal feelings in the matter we can try and understand the whole picture.

Once again, before you start your day, plan it out and see it in your mind's eye over and over again. This will give you the ability to be comfortable with any action you take because you have already worked out all of the options.

Pathway to an *Addiction Free* Lifestyle

Pathway to an *Addiction Free* Lifestyle

GROUP DISCUSSION

WEEK EIGHT

SESSION 1

SURVIVAL ROLES and COPING MECHANISMS

Throughout the past several weeks, we have discussed the importance of self-awareness, the significance of insight into anger management issues, and the roles our families may have played in our spiral into addiction and/or destructive behavior.

This group discussion will cover several areas of "Survival Roles" and "Coping Mechanisms". These areas include discussing ways to incorporate self-awareness, anger management, and family roles into the "Recovery and Social Wellness" techniques. These new life skills can and should be applied into your daily Life Plan.

We begin by examining the interpersonal problems associated with the family unit as it relates to family members being dependent on each other, and the roles that will eventually help the family reconstruct a functional family unit. The five (5) primary family survival roles are used as "Coping Mechanisms". These coping mechanisms are:

1. **Chief Enabler**-is identified as the family member that assumes primary responsibility for the chemically dependent family member. The chief enabler will shelter, protect, and even denies the dysfunctional aspects of a family member's alcohol/drug use.

2. **Family Hero**-is identified as the overachiever of the family. The family hero, who is usually the first born, is the responsible child or person in the family who plays the role as the savior who has somehow escaped the family's dysfunctional behavior patterns. In most cases, the hero often ignores his or her own personal feelings for so long, that these ignored or bottled-up feelings begin to have an adverse affect on that individual, turning into anger, resentment, and depression.

3. **Family Scapegoat**-is identified as the family member that diverts the family away from the real problems within the family. The scapegoat will always take the blame for all of the family's problems.

4. **The Lost Child**-is perhaps the most tragic role within the family unit. The lost child often identifies with the pain of their parents, and/or other siblings that are dealing with addiction or behavior problems. The lost child has an overwhelming desire to decrease the family's pain by not contributing to the family's problems, and taking on all of the family's pain. The family inadvertently reinforces the lost child's role within the family by ignoring the child's own needs, and continuing to depend on the child's acceptance of the family's problems. Eventually, the child will become overwhelmed with emotional issues resulting in the child either joining the family in their addictive or destructive behavior, or a complete mental breakdown.

5. **Family Mascot**-is identified as the family member that diverts attention from the family's dysfunctional issues and family pain by using humor, silliness, or even making fun of themselves, in order to keep the family from focusing on the real issues. The family mascot places a huge burden on themselves to keep a smile on everyone's face.

These coping mechanisms emphasize the need for the entire family to:

- Re-establish communication
- Work through old resentments
- Develop trust, and
- Strive to engage in a comfortable and rewarding relationship

A family free of substance abuse is far more than a family without drugs or alcohol in their lives. It is a family that has completely changed their way of thinking, acting, and communicating, which leads to an entirely different lifestyle from which they had been living.

What survival role did you play in your family? (check one)

( ) The Chief Enabler
( ) The Family Hero
( ) The Family Scapegoat
( ) The Lost Child
( ) The Family Mascot
( ) The Family Addict

Was your role in the family ( ) a survival role, ( ) a coping mechanism or ( ) both? Please give an explanation.

_____

_____

_____

_____

Did your survival role within your family unit become a vital element of your pathway to destructive behavior which led you to this program? ( ) YES ( ) NO Explain how?

_____

_____

_____

_____

Pathway to an *Addiction Free* Lifestyle

GROUP DISCUSSION

WEEK EIGHT

SESSION 1

SURVIVAL ROLES and COPING MECHANISMS

Survival roles and coping mechanisms correlate to, and are similar to Co-dependent variants. The signs and symptoms of co-dependence are so comprehensive and diverse that no individual will display every one. Co-dependents who are still in denial will often point to aspects of the disease which do not "fit" them, using such negative evidence to "prove" that they are not codependent or to minimize the extent of their co-dependence.

There are, however a collection of certain behaviors that are often seen in co-dependents. Codependents can often identify with a specific variant more than with the more general diagnosis of co-dependence. To the professional's eye all these variants are seen as being different expressions of the same underlying issues.

There are five (5) primary variants involved with co-dependency. These variants are:

1.) The Martyr

The martyr is the most common manifestation of co-dependence. Martyrs operate primarily on false pride. They take great pleasure from their capacity to put up with inconvenience, disappointment, and pain. They derive their self-worth from being able to fight the battle as much as from winning or losing. Martyrs deem it more important to be "right" than to be effective. Martyrs feel empty inside, but they are usually so busy being martyrs that they have little or no time to experience that emptiness, and what it means.

2.) The Persecutor

The persecutor is the exact opposite of the martyr. Persecutors harbor much of the rage and bitterness which martyrs cannot allow themselves to feel. Although their own behavior often seems out of control, they focus on what everyone else is doing wrong. Rather than dealing with their own unhappiness, they externalize it and blame it on the actions of others. While martyrs take full responsibility for feeling miserable, persecutors take no responsibility for theirs. While martyrs push themselves to work harder to feel better, persecutors push others to provide them with security and peace of mind. Both overestimate the impact they have on those around them. Neither knows the difference between what they can and cannot control. The martyr keeps trying to manipulate others by being good; and the persecutor keeps trying to manipulate others with anger and guilt.

3.) The Co-Conspirator

Some co-dependents continually undermine the chemical dependents' efforts to attain sobriety. Although this seems counter-productive from the outside, it can make sense from within the co-dependent's world. Co-dependents become attached to the identities they develop within the actively chemically dependent family system. The thought of having to develop a new identity, a requirement for functioning within a recovering family, causes considerable anxiety. Rather than change, they become co-conspirators or enablers. Most co-conspirators are offended by the mere suggestion that a family member may have a problem. It is a painful irony that many coconspirators become professionals in the Co-Dependency field out of concern for the harm that drugs and alcohol are doing to this country and to family life in general. The words "in general" are key to understanding this phenomenon. Co-conspirators know that chemical dependence is a "bad thing"; they simply are not willing to recognize its presence close to home. However, there are some co-conspirators that are capable of acknowledging that a family member is chemically dependent, and even of expressing concern about that person. But then they turn around and offer him or her drugs, or a drink, volunteering to stop at the store to buy more alcohol. When confronted with the inconsistency of their behavior, they deny that it is contributing to the problem or claim that they can't act any differently.

4.) The Drinking (or Drugging) Partner

Co-dependents are at risk for becoming chemically dependent. Their lifestyle and belief system are already so close to those of chemical dependence that it is easy to slip into addiction. Many co-dependents believe that the best way to "connect" with a chemically dependent family member is by joining in. Eventually they become chemically dependent as well. Sometimes the co-dependents eyes are opened when he or she simply can't keep up with the chemical dependent's consumption of alcohol and/or drugs. This is the point at which a healthy person would start confronting the chemical dependent with this knowledge. For active co-dependents, however, this is too risky. Instead, they back off on their own using and bury their heads in the sand, hoping that the chemical dependent will someday do the same.

5.) The Apathetic Co-Dependent

Some co-dependents simply stop caring. They become so thoroughly demoralized that they sink into an emotional stupor, like concentration camp inmates resigned to their fate. Apathy may bring a certain peace or calm, but it is devoid of any sense of hope or meaning in life. This is especially distressing when there are children in the home. When Dad or Mom gives up, there is no one left to model healthy responses to the chaos and insanity of living with chemical dependence. For severe apathetic co-dependents, suicide becomes a realistic and acceptable option. They may take their own lives actively and directly, or passively and indirectly, by doing nothing to avoid an accident, for example, or by refusing to see a doctor at the onset of disease.

What is important to realize is that co-dependence wears many faces. Doubtless there are other variants that those described above. And there are no "rules" determining which ones codependents may manifest and when: the martyr may become the persecutor; the co-conspirator may become apathetic, and so on.

Pathway to an *Addiction Free* Lifestyle

Oversimplification of the concept is an ever-present danger, and describing "typical" behaviors or roles is a sure way of falling into that trap. The absence of any (or all) of these recognizable variants should not be taken as evidence that co-dependence does not exist.

Pathway to an *Addiction Free* Lifestyle

PERSONAL DEVELOPMENT ASSIGNMENT

WEEK EIGHT

SESSION 1

COMPLETE YOUR LIFE PLAN OUTLINE

The Personal Development Assignment will be to complete your Life Plan Outline. This is done by looking over all your completed assignments and listing all the information. This will give you a clear road map for success and give you the ability to understand the problems that will enter your journey. Now you have the capability of dealing with them or to get the help you need for every direction and resource available. By being able to handle your problems in a very constructive manner you will not enter that road of feeling helpless or hopeless. These feelings, as we all know leads us back to self-destruction and substance abuse.

So please complete your Life Plan Outline at this time.

Pathway to an *Addiction Free* Lifestyle

Pathway to an *Addiction Free* Lifestyle

GROUP DISCUSSION

WEEK EIGHT

SESSION 2

RELAPSE PREVENTION PLAN

This group will look at comprehensive relapse prevention plan outline G-1 to include how and where to find and obtain a sponsor. As well as the different post-parole programs and support systems that needs to be in place. These important issues need to be clear, concise, and honestly brought into the open for a clear understanding of them. Then we will do a complete program overview and the individuals requesting counselors will be assigned to help them with the continued relapse prevention plan and social roles.

Graduation Day!

Pathway to an *Addiction Free* Lifestyle

PARTICIPANT EVALUATION FORM (COMPLETION)

Group# _____ Participant Name: _____

1. Write something you learned about yourself during the Workshops:

_____
_____
_____
_____

2. Write about something you learned in general.

_____
_____
_____
_____

3. What are some of the most valuable aspects of this experience?

_____
_____
_____
_____

4. How do you think what you've gained here will affect your life?

_____
_____
_____
_____

5. What I didn't like about the program?

6. What do you feel can be improved?

7. How do you think this will help in long term recovery?

APPENDIX

'A'

PARTICIPATION

&

CONFIDENTIAL AGREEMENT

Pathway to an *Addiction Free* Lifestyle

Pathway to an *Addiction Free* Lifestyle

PARTICIPATION & CONFIDENTIAL AGREEMENT

Name: _____
                Last   First   Middle

Address: _____

I, _____, hereby agree to the following terms of participation
        (Print Full Name)

in the 'Breaking Free' Drug and Behavior Self-Awareness Treatment Program.

Guidelines that I must follow: (check each one after reading and understanding fully)

1. I will not repeat any personal information concerning anyone that is participating in any group that I attend to any outside person and / or group.

2. I will not pass on any assignments, homework or otherwise, to anyone outside of the group.

3. I will turn in all Personal Development Assignments on the date required.

4. I understand that if I miss any sessions I will be subjected to program review.

I understand that such a contract and disclosure are necessary for the integrity and coordination of services relating to my treatment and process of my 'Sobriety and Social Wellness'.

This consent shall be valid from _____ to _____.

_____   _____
(Participant Printed Name)   (Participant Signature & Date)

Pathway to an *Addiction Free* Lifestyle

Pathway to an *Addiction Free* Lifestyle

APPENDIX

'B'

INITIAL ASSESSMENT

Pathway to an *Addiction Free* Lifestyle

Pathway to an *Addiction Free* Lifestyle

INITIAL ASSESSMENT

1. Name: _____
                Last   First   Middle

2 Home address: _____

3. Birth date: _____

4. Have you been incarcerated: Yes / No   How many times: _____

5. Married _____   Single _____   Divorced _____   Separated _____   Widowed _____

6. Education Status: _____   No formal schooling: _____   Completed grade: _____

High School/GED: _____   Some college: (No Degree) _____   AA/AS Degree: _____

BA Degree: _____   Master's Degree: _____   PhD: _____

7. Have you ever completed a trade and/or vocational school: Yes _____   No _____

    a. Were you ever in special education classes: Yes _____   No _____

    b. Do you have a problem with reading or vocabulary: Yes _____   No _____

    c. Is English your second language: Yes _____   No _____

8.   Have you ever been arrested for substance abuse:

    a. If juvenile arrest, were you ever placed in:

        Juvenile Hall: _____   CYA: _____   Group Home: _____

        Boys Ranch: _____   In House Placement: _____   Boot Camp: _____

    b. What were your first charges:

_____

_____

    c. List all other charges related to substance abuse:

_____

_____

Pathway to an *Addiction Free* Lifestyle

9. Were you ever expelled from school as a child: Yes _____ No _____

10. Have you ever been fired or terminated from a job: Yes _____ No _____

    Why: _____
    _____

11. Ever been employed for six (6) months at the same job: Yes _____ No _____

12. If yes, what was your job time base: Full Time: _____ Part Time: _____

13. Age of first drug/alcohol use: _____

14. Number of years of problem usage: _____

    a. First substance that you used: _____

    b. List all other drugs you have used: _____
    _____

    c. How used: Intravenous: _____   Smoked: _____

                    Snorted: _____   Ingested: _____

    14. Primary drug of choice:

        N/A: _____   Alcohol: _____   Cocaine: _____   Crack: _____

        Hallucinogenic: _____   Heroin: _____   Marijuana: _____

        Methamphetamines: _____   Other: _____

16. Second drug of choice: _____

17. Previous treatment: Yes _____ No _____

    a. Residential treatment program(s): Yes _____ No _____

    Where: _____

    b. Outpatient treatment program(s): Yes _____ No _____

    Where: _____

    c. Jail based program(s): Yes _____ No _____

B-4

Pathway to an *Addiction Free* Lifestyle

Where: _____

    d. Prison based program(s):   Yes _____   No _____

Where: _____

18. Attended 12-Step Meetings: Yes _____   No _____

    Which do you prefer: AA: _____   NA: _____   Other: _____

19. Employment: Yes _____   No _____

    a. What type of work have you done in the past:

    _____

    _____

    b. What type of work would you like to do:

    _____

    _____

20. Are you a Veteran: Yes _____   No _____

    Branch of Service: _____

    Discharge status: General: _____   Honorable: _____

                              Dishonorable: _____   Other: _____

21. Medical History: _____

    _____

    _____

    Current medical problem(s): _____

    _____

    _____

22. Mental health history: _____

Pathway to an *Addiction Free* Lifestyle

_____

_____

Ever had formal treatment: _____

_____

_____

Reason for treatment: _____

_____

_____

Past diagnosis: _____

_____

_____

Past medications: _____

_____

_____

Current prescribed medications: _____

_____

_____

Suicide attempts: Yes: _____   No: _____

If yes, please explain: _____

_____

_____

23.   History of any other abuses of any kind: Yes: _____   No: _____

If so, Please explain: _____

_____

APPENDIX

'C'

VIDEOS and DVDs

Pathway to an *Addiction Free* Lifestyle

VIDEOS and DVDs

1. Killing Time (HIV/AIDS)
2. Hepatitis 'C' Inside and Out
3. Magic Johnson's HIV Education in Prison
4. Discovery Channel's: Understanding Bacteria
5. Discovery Channel's: Understanding Viruses
6. The Silent Killer: Hepatitis Awareness for Offenders

Pathway to an *Addiction Free* Lifestyle

APPENDIX

'D'

HANDOUTS and LISTINGS

Pathway to an *Addiction Free* Lifestyle

Pathway to an *Addiction Free* Lifestyle

HANDOUTS and LISTINGS

1. Living with MRSA
2. HCV Hepatitis 'C' Basic
3. HCV Hepatitis '13': What You Need to Know
4. Tattoo and You
5. Beyond Fear: HIV
6. Hepatitis 'C' Treatment

Pathway to an *Addiction Free* Lifestyle

Pathway to an *Addiction Free* Lifestyle

APPENDIX

'E'

EXIT PLAN / PLAN FOR

POST RELEASE

Pathway to an *Addiction Free* Lifestyle

Pathway to an *Addiction Free* Lifestyle

EXIT PLAN

Name: _____
        (Last)   (First)   (Middle Initial)

GOALS:

1. _____
2. _____
3. _____
4. _____
5. _____
6. _____

ACTION STEPS:

1. _____
2. _____
3. _____
4. _____
5. _____
6. _____

Date Plan Written: _____

Date Plan to be Reviewed: _____

_____   _____
Participant Signature   Specialist Signature

Pathway to an *Addiction Free* Lifestyle

Pathway to an *Addiction Free* Lifestyle

PLAN FOR POST RELEASE

During Initial Assessment, inmate and case manager will identify resources needed by participant. Case Manager will prioritize area of need from 1 (low) to 10 (immediate, urgent need).

_____ Substance Abuse Services:

    _____ Residential Treatment   _____ Outpatient Treatment

    _____ 12-Step Meeting   _____ Detox

    _____ Clean and Sober Living:

_____ Housing:

    _____ Emergency Shelter   _____ Low Income Housing

    _____ Independent Living   _____ Board and Care

    _____ Section 8   _____ Seasons of Sharing

    _____ Utilities

_____ Basic Needs:

    _____ ID Card   _____ Food

    _____ Clothing   _____ Transportation

    _____ Duplicate Social Security Card

_____ Financial Aid:

    _____ Social Security   _____ Public Assistance

    _____ Unemployment   _____ Consumer Credit Services

_____ Education:

    _____ Literacy Tutoring   _____ Adult Education

    _____ Vocational Schools   _____ College

Pathway to an *Addiction Free* Lifestyle

_____ Health and Mental Health Care:

    _____ Crisis Mental Health   _____ Emergency Health Care

    _____ Health Insurance   _____ Prescription Refills

    _____ Primary Health Care   _____ Dental Care

    _____ Veteran's Administration

_____ Employment:

    _____ Job Training   _____ Vocational Rehabilitation

    _____ Apprenticeships   _____ Full/Par-Time Opportunities

    _____ EDD

_____ Child Services:

    _____ Parenting Classes   _____ Child Care

    _____ Pre-School   _____ WIC

    _____ Youth Drug Treatment   _____ Recreation

    _____ Big Brothers/Sisters   _____ Supervised Visits

_____ Legal Assistance:

    _____ Child Support   _____ Child Custody

    _____ Divorce   _____ Traffic Fines

_____ Counseling:

    _____ Anger Management   _____ Family

    _____ Individual   _____ Domestic Violence

_____ Other: If not listed, please describe service(s) needed.

_____

_____

_____

APPENDIX

'F'

MIND MAPPING

Pathway to an *Addiction Free* Lifestyle

Pathway to an *Addiction Free* Lifestyle

MIND MAPPING

<u>WITH SUBSTANCE ABUSE</u>　　　　　　　　　<u>WITHOUT SUBSTANCE ABUSE</u>

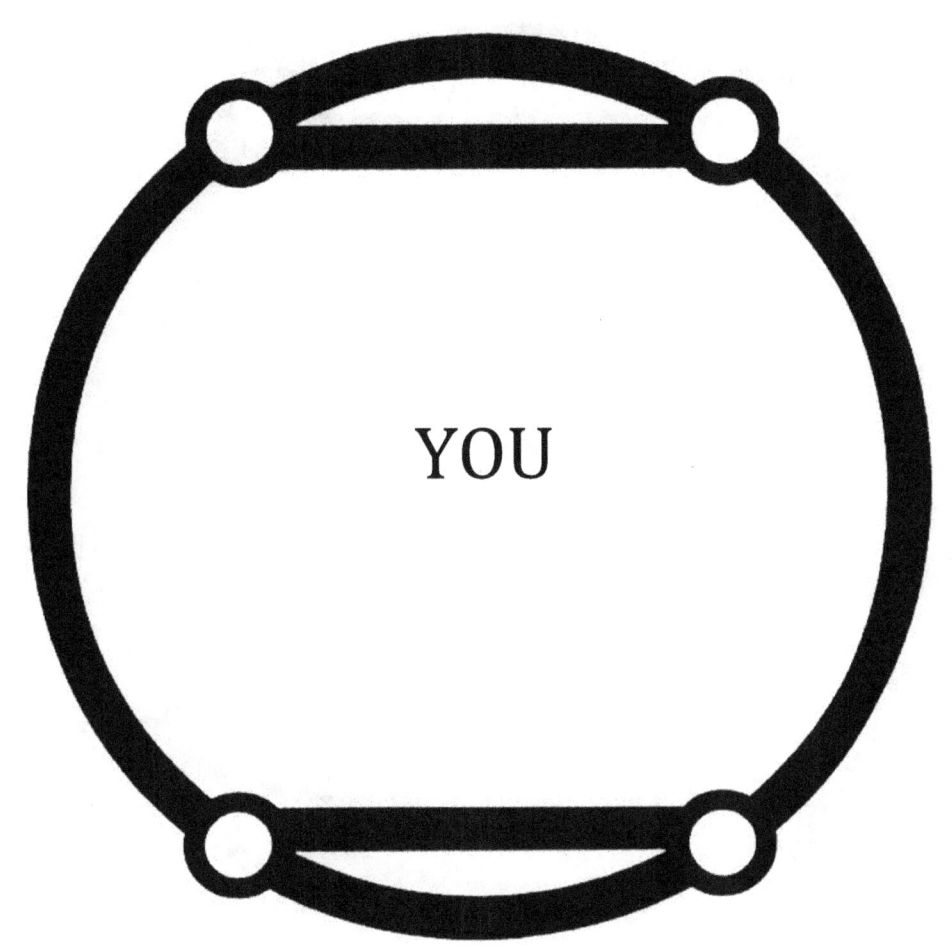

F-3

Pathway to an *Addiction Free* Lifestyle
MIND MAPPING

WITH SUBSTANCE ABUSE   WITHOUT SUBSTANCE ABUSE

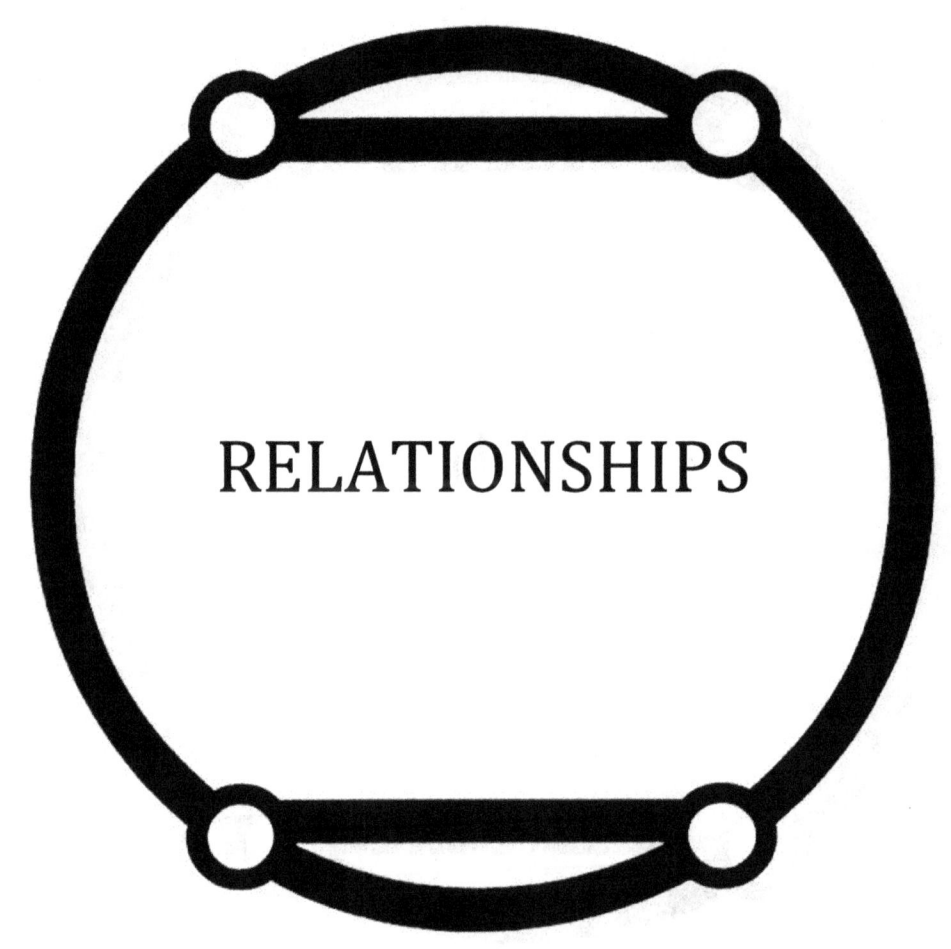

Pathway to an *Addiction Free* Lifestyle

MIND MAPPING

<u>WITH SUBSTANCE ABUSE</u>   <u>WITHOUT SUBSTANCE ABUSE</u>

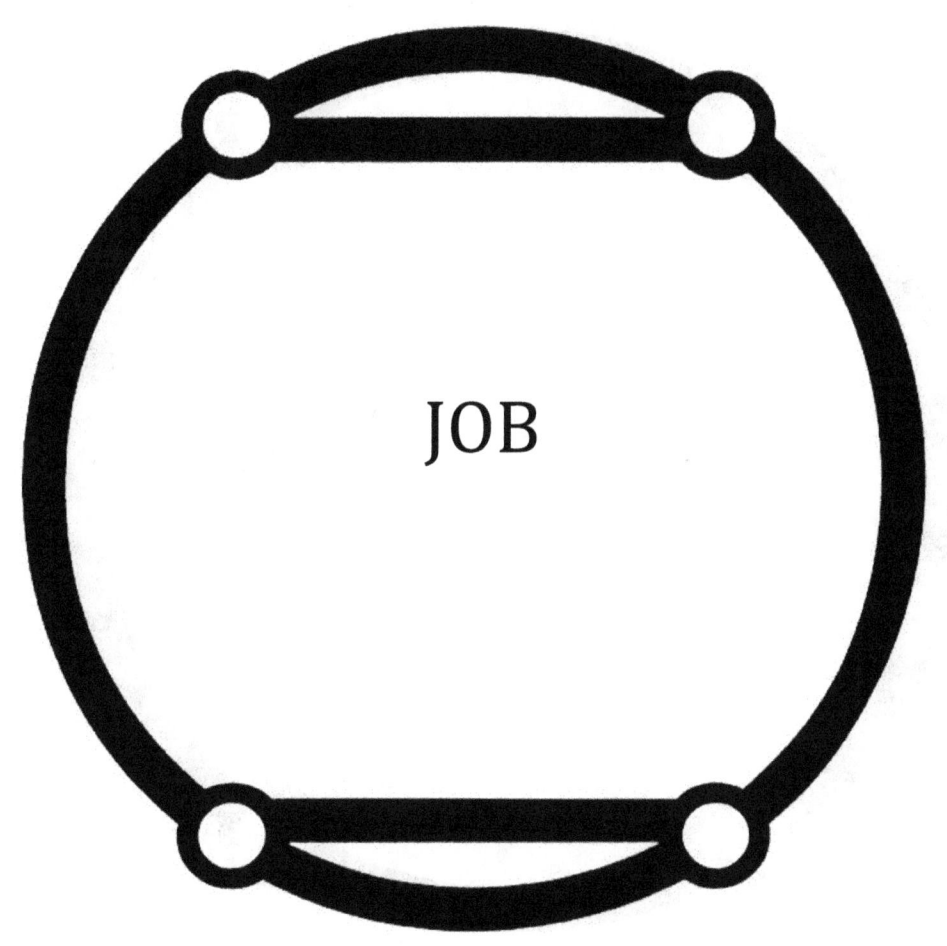

Pathway to an *Addiction Free* Lifestyle

MIND MAPPING

<u>WITH SUBSTANCE ABUSE</u>　　　　　　　　　　　<u>WITHOUT SUBSTANCE ABUSE</u>

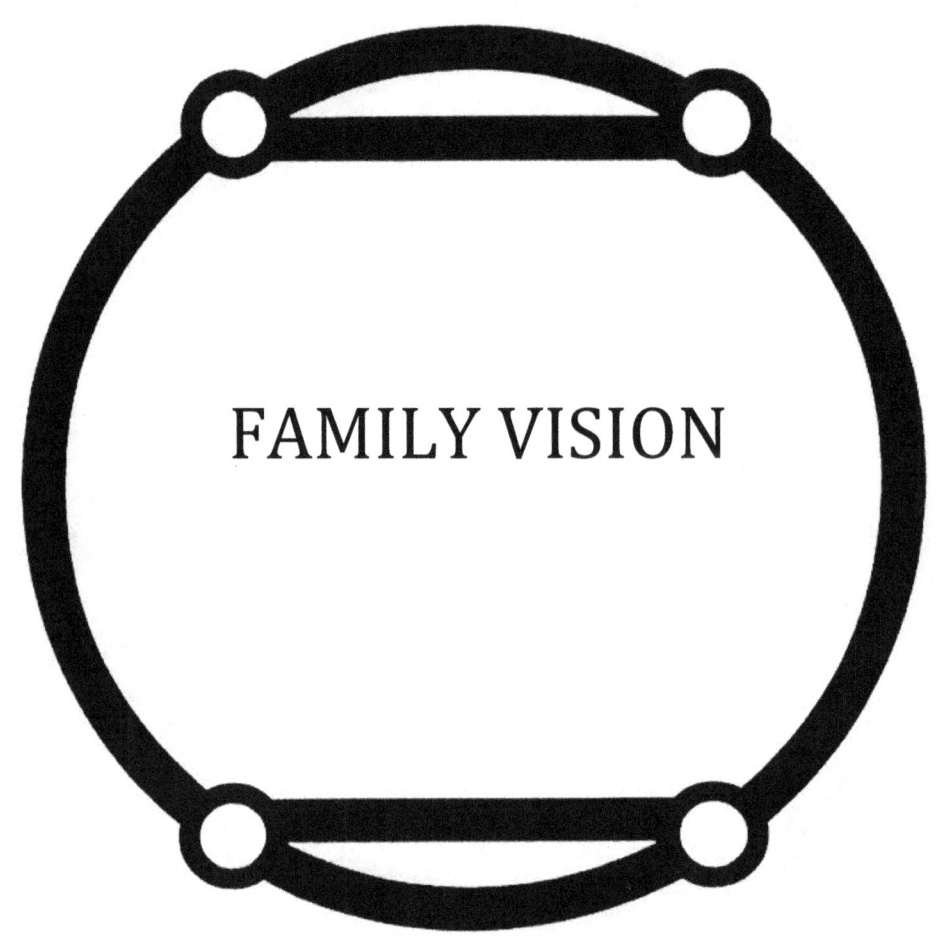

Pathway to an *Addiction Free* Lifestyle

MIND MAPPING

<u>WITH SUBSTANCE ABUSE</u>   <u>WITHOUT SUBSTANCE ABUSE</u>

Pathway to an *Addiction Free* Lifestyle

MIND MAPPING

<u>WITH SUBSTANCE ABUSE</u>   <u>WITHOUT SUBSTANCE ABUSE</u>

Pathway to an *Addiction Free* Lifestyle

APPENDIX

'G'

LIFE PLANNING

&

RELAPSE PREVENTION PLAN

Pathway to an *Addiction Free* Lifestyle

Pathway to an *Addiction Free* Lifestyle

WHAT IS DENIAL?

Webster defines "denial" as saying no: Contradicting, refusing to believe or accept, and abstinence from desired things. All these definitions fit with chemical dependency or abuse in that there is a protection of self, consciously or unconsciously, against unacceptable reality.

In general, denial is a psychological mechanism or process that humans use to protect themselves from something threatening them. This process blocks awareness from the conscious mind. Often denial is seen as lying, which can be the truth when practiced purposefully. For example: a person has a positive U.A. and knows they used, yet tells everyone they did not use.

1. **Denial is a core component of the illness**: The development of a denial system is a fundamental and essential feature of chemical dependence. As a primary symptom of the disease, denial develops strength as symptoms, and/or harmful consequences increase. To some extent denial is found in all persons who have chemical abuse or chemical dependency. Through progressively impaired judgment, which leads to greater self-delusion, denial becomes a fatal aspect of chemical dependence, locking one into increasingly destructive patterns. The denial system is psychologically developed while the addict/alcoholic is actively using. However, the denial system which permits the addict/alcoholic stops using. It is this denial system which permits the addict/alcoholic to ignore relapse warning signs and feedback from others, and often leads the addict/alcoholic back to addictive use.

2. **Denial is Automatic**: Usually denial in its various forms is not deliberate lying or willful deception; it is an unconscious psychological maneuver for self-protection. In most addicts/alcoholics there is loss of touch with the truth, reality, if you will. The denial system distorts reality to such an extent that an addict/alcoholic is no longer capable of accurate self-awareness. This self-delusion can range from extreme grandiosity to utter defeat.

3. **Denial is progressive**: As the illness of chemical dependence progresses, the denial system becomes more pervasive and entrenched.

4. **Denial has many faces**: Denial is a system of many psychological defenses and maneuvers that are utilized to protect one from the realization that they are not in control. These defenses and maneuvers, all distorting reality, take many forms. Some of the most common forms are listed on the next page.

Exercise # 1 — Step-down Relapse Prevention Packet.

A. **Simple Denial**: Maintaining that something is not so, when in reality, it is a fact.

(Example: The active addict/alcoholic denying that chemical usage is a problem. Example: The addict/alcoholic in recovery — denying that working 60 hours a week is threatening their recovery when there is evidence that it is and/or others perceive and discuss it as a problem.).

Pathway to an *Addiction Free* Lifestyle

List at least one example of the above forms of denial that you have utilized since becoming clean and sober. List the circumstances and your behavior surrounding the circumstances. What was the threatening reality you were attempting to avoid?

_____

_____

_____

_____

B. Minimizing: Admitting to some degree that there is a problem, yet making the problem appear less serious than it really is. (Example: The active addict/alcoholic — "So, I had a little too much last night." Of course no mention of the recurrent pattern of having too much is made. Example: The active addict/alcoholic in recovery — "So, I haven't spoken to my sponsor this week, I haven't had any problems." Of course no mention of the negative attitude he/she has been exhibiting is made.).

List at least one example of the above forms of denial that you have utilized since becoming clean and sober. List the circumstances and your behavior surrounding the circumstances. What was the threatening reality you were attempting to avoid?

_____

_____

_____

_____

C. Blaming or Projection: Denial of personal responsibility for certain behavior and placing responsibility on other persons, places, things, or situations. (Example: The active addict/alcoholic — You would use too if you had my spouse, kids, jog, parents, problems, or some other excuse." Example: The addict/alcoholic in recovery — "You would be angry, frustrated, depressed, etc... if you had to put up with my treatment, probation officer, wife, job, boss, finances, or some other excuse.").

List at least one example of the above forms of denial that you have utilized since becoming clean and sober. List the circumstances and your behavior surrounding the circumstances. What was the threatening reality you were attempting to avoid?

_____

_____

_____

_____

D. Rationalizing: Offering excuses, alibis, and justifications for behaviors. These excuses serve to place explanations on things other than chemical usage or personal responsibility for unacceptable behavior. The behavior is not denied, the explanation is simply inaccurate. (Example: The active alcoholic addict — "Yes, I fell and broke my leg because the chair had been moved." No mention of being under the influence of chemicals. Example: The alcoholic/addict in recovery — "Yes, I have missed meetings because I have been working to pay my bills." No mention that he/she just bought an expensive home entertainment center that they could not afford.).

List at least one example of the above forms of denial that you have utilized since becoming clean and sober. List the circumstances and your behavior surrounding the circumstances. What was the threatening reality you were attempting to avoid?

_____

_____

_____

_____

E. Intellectualizing: Avoiding emotional or personal responsibility or the problem by using generalizations, intellectual analysis or theorizing. (Example: The active alcoholic/addict — My behavior when using chemicals is okay when I eat before drinking, it is not to stuffy, everything is going okay at home or work, if someone else drives or I don't hurt anyone bit myself...etc..." Example: The alcoholic/addict in recovery — "My inappropriate behavior is okay as long as I tell my sponsor about it, go to meetings, pray or stay clean and sober.")

List at least one example of the above forms of denial that you have utilized since becoming clean and sober. List the circumstances and your behavior surrounding the circumstances. What was the threatening reality you were attempting to avoid?

F. Diversion: Changing the subject to avoid threatening topics. (Example: The active addict/alcoholic — "John, I am very concerned about how much you drank last night." "Yes, I was tired normally I can handle it. What do you think we need to do about the upcoming meeting about proposed office changes?" Example: The addict/alcoholic in recovery — "John, I am very concerned about your behavior and attitude lately." "Yes, I have been tired but I'm okay. Hey, did you see the ballgame on Sunday?")

List at least one example of the above forms of denial that you have utilized since becoming clean and sober. List the circumstances and your behavior surrounding the circumstances. What was the threatening reality you were attempting to avoid?

_____

_____

G. Hostility: Becoming angry or irritable when reference is made to chemical use or other problematic behaviors. Hostile reactions tend to back people off. People learn quickly to avoid topics that create angry or irritable responses or will change the subject to avoid wrath. Not many people enjoy angry conversations and thus avoid some important subjects. (Example: The active addict/alcoholic and the addict/alcoholic in recovery — "You don't know what you're talking about. Mind your own business. Stop taking my inventory. Who are you to be telling me what to do? You don't understand, so forget it." Or simply storming off and refusing to discuss subjects.).

List at least one example of the above forms of denial that you have utilized since becoming clean and sober. List the circumstances and your behavior surrounding the circumstances. What was the threatening reality you were attempting to avoid?

_____

_____

_____

_____

IDENTIFYING HIGH RISK SITUATIONS

A high risk situation is any situation that is likely to activate relapse warning signs, triggers, or cravings to use. There are many possible high risk situations such as: Being around old places, old people, and old things, getting fired, getting divorced, having an argument, having an accident, and so forth. It is important to know what situations could activate relapse warning signs, triggers, and cravings to use, so that you can create a plan for what to do instead.

Exercise # 2 — Step-down Relapse Prevention Packet

Part A. Think of two past situations that activated relapse warning signs, triggers, or cravings to use.

Past situation #1:

_____

_____

_____

_____

Pathway to an *Addiction Free* Lifestyle

What are the chances you will experience a situation like this within the next 3 months? (Circle the most correct answer)

    ALMOST CERTAIN   HIGH   LOW   VERY LOW

If you do experience a situation like this, what are the chances that you will use?

    ALMOST CERTAIN   HIGH   LOW   VERY LOW

Past situation # 2:

_____

_____

_____

_____

What are the chances you will experience a situation like this within the next 3 months? (Circle the most correct answer)

    ALMOST CERTAIN   HIGH   LOW   VERY LOW

If you do experience a situation like this, what are the chances that you will use?

    ALMOST CERTAIN   HIGH   LOW   VERY LOW

Part B. Think of two present situations that could activate relapse warning signs, triggers, or cravings to use. Present situation # 1:

_____

_____

_____

_____

What are the chances you will experience a situation like this within the next 3 months? (Circle the most correct answer)

    ALMOST CERTAIN   HIGH   LOW   VERY LOW

If you do experience a situation like this, what are the chances that you will use?

    ALMOST CERTAIN   HIGH   LOW   VERY LOW

Pathway to an *Addiction Free* Lifestyle

Present situation # 2:

_____

_____

_____

_____

What are the chances you will experience a situation like this within the next 3 months? (Circle the most correct answer)

      ALMOST CERTAIN   HIGH   LOW   VERY LOW

If you do experience a situation like this, what are the chances that you will use?

      ALMOST CERTAIN   HIGH   LOW   VERY LOW

Part C. Think of two future situations that could activate relapse warning signs, triggers, or cravings to use.

Program Future situation # 1:

_____

_____

_____

_____

What are the chances you will experience a situation like this within the next 3 months? (Circle the most correct answer)

      ALMOST CERTAIN   HIGH   LOW   VERY LOW

If you do experience a situation like this, what are the chances that you will use?

      ALMOST CERTAIN   HIGH   LOW   VERY LOW

Future situation # 2:

_____

_____

_____

What are the chances you will experience a situation like this within the next 3 months? (Circle the most correct answer)

ALMOST CERTAIN   HIGH   LOW   VERY LOW

If you do experience a situation like this, what are the chances that you will use?

ALMOST CERTAIN   HIGH   LOW   VERY LOW

DEALING WITH CRAVINGS

Having cravings and urges for alcohol/drugs is normal for anyone who has habitually used alcohol/drugs and is now making an effort to remain clean and sober. No matter how motivated you are to stay off alcohol/drugs, at some point you will probably have a sudden desire to use. It is essential that you not act on the craving or use them as an excuse to get high. Cravings can threaten your ability to stay clean and sober especially if you misinterpret them or fail to deal with them. For example: You may feel guilty and disappointed by cravings because you see them as sign of not recovering "right". You may try to ignore them because you feel that you shouldn't be having thoughts about wanting to use. Or you may assume, incorrectly, that you shouldn't be having thoughts about wanting to use. Or you may assume, incorrectly, that once a craving starts it will inevitably get so strong that you will not be able to resist the impulse to use.

The purpose of this section is to educate you about cravings, and to help you develop a specific plan for preventing cravings from leading to alcohol/drug use. Ignoring or denying cravings is a very poor defense against them. Specific action must be taken in dealing with cravings to prevent them from leading to alcohol/drug use.

Exercise # 3 — Step-down Relapse Prevention Packet

1. Cravings are impulsive or spontaneous desires to use alcohol/drugs. They are often accompanied by feelings of anxiety or restlessness. Thoughts of how good it would feel to get high, and a hunger or compulsion to use. Cravings are a natural result of chronically and habitually using alcohol/drugs to alter your mood.

Think about when you have had cravings in the past and answer the following questions:

   a. Describe how the craving felt emotionally, mentally, and physically.

   _____

   _____

   _____

b. Describe what you were thinking during the craving.

_____

_____

_____

_____

c. Describe what your actions were during the cravings.

_____

_____

_____

_____

2. Cravings are usually triggered by something — people, places, things, feelings — associated with your alcohol/drug use. Cravings can also be triggered by using dreams.

List People, places, things, and circumstances that are likely to trigger your cravings now.

People:	Places:	Things:	Circumstances:
_____	_____	_____	_____
_____	_____	_____	_____
_____	_____	_____	_____
_____	_____	_____	_____
_____	_____	_____	_____
_____	_____	_____	_____
_____	_____	_____	_____
_____	_____	_____	_____
_____	_____	_____	_____

Pathway to an *Addiction Free* Lifestyle

_____   _____   _____   _____

_____   _____   _____   _____

3. <u>When cravings appear to be totally unrelated to what's going on around you, they are usually caused by what's going on inside of you — your emotional state.</u>

List thoughts, feelings, and actions, that are, likely to trigger your cravings now.

Thoughts: _____

_____

_____

Feelings: _____

_____

_____

Actions: _____

_____

_____

4. <u>Cravings tend to be strongest and occur most frequently in the first weeks after you have stopped using alcohol/drugs. Cravings diminish as abstinence continues. Using alcohol/drugs even after a long abstinence renews cravings and increases their strength and frequency.</u>

Think Beyond the High:

Describe what excuses you have thought of, to justify your drug/alcohol use:

_____

_____

_____

_____

Describe the immediate negative consequences to using:

_____

G-11

Pathway to an *Addiction Free* Lifestyle

_____
_____
_____

Describe the immediate positive consequences to not using:

_____
_____
_____
_____

Describe the delayed negative consequences to using:

_____
_____
_____
_____

Describe the delayed negative consequences to not using:

_____
_____
_____
_____

5. <u>The intensity of a craving does not fade merely with the passage of time, but as a result of not reinforcing with alcohol/drug use</u>. Cravings lose power, little by little, each time you respond to the craving by not using alcohol/drugs. This process is known as extinction. Complete abstinence from all mood altering chemicals is necessary for complete extinction of cravings. (An exception to this can be if a person is on a medication prescribed by a psychiatrist or doctor to control emotional or mental disorders. In this case, not taking medications as prescribed could produce alcohol/drug cravings.) It is dangerous to intentionally expose yourself to your alcohol/drug triggers. Example: Going to bars with the intention of drinking only cokes, or shopping in a liquor store. This is likely to backfire; eventually, these cravings will overwhelm you and cause a relapse.

Leave or Change the Situation:

Pathway to an *Addiction Free* Lifestyle

Describe positive activities you could immediately do in response to a craving:

_____
_____
_____
_____

6. <u>Cravings are always temporary and tend to disappear quickly, especially when immediate action is taken to short-circuit them</u>. Most cravings are like waves — they peak, stay there for a short period of time, and then rapidly fall off. Get Help:

List names and telephone numbers of people, groups, and/or organizations you have regular contact with, and that are a part of your social support system.

NAME	TELEPHONE NUMBER	CONTACTED HOW OFTEN?
_____	_____	_____
_____	_____	_____
_____	_____	_____
_____	_____	_____
_____	_____	_____
_____	_____	_____
_____	_____	_____
_____	_____	_____
_____	_____	_____
_____	_____	_____

List names and telephone numbers of people, groups, and/or organizations, which could be a part of your social support system.

NAME	TELEPHONE NUMBER
_____	_____

Pathway to an *Addiction Free* Lifestyle

_____   _____
_____   _____
_____   _____
_____   _____
_____   _____
_____   _____
_____   _____
_____   _____
_____   _____

Delay making a decision:

Describe what thoughts and actions might assist you to ride out a craving.

Thoughts: _____

_____

_____

Actions: _____

_____

_____

RELAPSE WARNING SIGNS

The following is a list of common relapse warning signs that often lead to relapse, if not dealt with appropriately. These symptoms are also known as "stinking thinking". Most addicts/alcoholics will have relapse warning signs as a normal part of their disease process. However, if warning signs are not dealt with, they can lead an addict/alcoholic to relapse. This is why it is important for an addict/alcoholic to be aware of these symptoms. A weekly inventory of relapse warning signs, might prevent some relapses.

Exercise # 4 — Step-down Relapse Prevention Packet

1. Read through the following list of relapse warning signs. Circle the warning signs you can relate to.

Pathway to an *Addiction Free* Lifestyle

EXHAUSTION: Allowing yourself to become overly tired or in poor health. Some addicts/alcoholics are also prone to work additions, perhaps in an effort to make up for lost time. Good health and enough rest are important. If you feel well, you are apt to think well. Feel poorly, and your thinking is apt to deteriorate. Feel bad long enough and you might begin to think using a little couldn't make it any worse.

DISHONESTY: This begins with a pattern of unnecessary little lies and deceits with fellow workers, family, friends, sponsor, and support group. Then comes the important lies to yourself. This is called rationalizing, minimizing and denying. This can include making excuses for not doing what you need to do or for doing what you know you should not do.

IMPATIENCE: Things are not happening fast enough. Or, others are not doing what they should do, what you think they should do or what you want them to do.

ARGUMENTATIVENESS: Arguing small and ridiculous points of view indicates a need to always be right, rather than a willingness to work for a solution. "Why don't you be reasonable and agree with me?" Creating disharmony in this fashion is looking for an excuse to use.

DEPRESSION: Unreasonable and unaccountable despair may occur in cycles and should be dealt with — talked about.

FRUSTRATION: At people, places, things, and situations because things may not be going your way. Remember things will not always go your way and that you are powerless over people, places, and things.

SELF-PITY: The Charlie Brown syndrome "Why is everybody always picking on me". Self-pity is different from sadness; you become a victim in self-pity and blame others for your situation and feelings. "Why do these things always happen to me?" "Why must I do this or that?" "Nobody appreciates what I am doing." "Why am I an addict/alcoholic?" Self-pity is an indication that there is something you're not doing that you need to be doing to care for your sobriety and usually indicates a need to change your thinking. Much resentment is based in nothing more than self-pity.

COCKINESS: Got it made; no longer fears drinking. Going or planning to go to drinking situations. Do this often enough and it will wear down your defenses. This also includes not being involved with your support group or staying in contact with a sponsor and higher power. You begin to believe that since you have made a decision not to drink or use that you do not need anyone else.

COMPLACENCY: "Using was the furthest thing from my mind." Not drinking was no longer a conscious thought either. It is dangerous to let up on defenses because everything is going well. To have a little fear is a good thing. More relapses occur when things are going well than otherwise.

EXPECTING TOO MUCH FROM OTHERS: "I've changed; why can't they." It's a plus if they do change, but it is still your problem if they don't. They may not trust you and are looking for further proof. You cannot expect others to change just because you have. Others are simply human also and make mistakes the same as you.

LETTING UP ON DISCIPLINES: This can stem from complacency, cockiness, or boredom. You cannot afford to be bored with you program. The cost of relapse is too great.

USE OF MOOD ALTERING CHEMICALS: You may feel a need to ease things by using other drugs and your friends may go along with you. You may believe that since you never had a problem with drugs or this particular drug or because this drug is not addictive, that this is allowable. For an addict using alcohol may look like an acceptable solution. This is the most subtle way to relapse. An addict can easily become an alcoholic and visa versa. Also once you compromise your sobriety it is not a long jump to begin using your drug of choice most especially when your judgment is impaired. Remember you will be cheating and cannot claim sobriety. (The exception to this is if you are on prescription medication for a mental or emotional disorder. In this case not taking your medication as prescribed can jeopardize your sobriety.)

WANTING TOO MUCH: Do not set goals you cannot reach with normal effort. Do not expect too much. It is always great when good things happen you are not expecting. You will get what you need as long as you do your best to do the next right thing. However, you may not get things as soon as you think you should. Be aware of magical thinking and focus on what is real today. "Happiness is not having what you want, but is wanting what you have."

FORGETTING GRATITUDE: You may be looking negatively on your life. Concentrating on problems that still are not totally correct. Nobody wants to be a Pollyanna, but it is good to remember where you started from and how much better life is now.

"IT CAN'T HAPPEN TO ME": This is dangerous thinking. Almost anything can happen to you and is more likely if you become careless. Remember you have a progressive disease, and you will be in worse shape if you relapse.

OMNIPOTENCE: This is a feeling that results from a combination of many of the above, a feeling of unlimited power. You may have all the answers for yourself and others. Relapse is probably imminent unless drastic changes take place.

2. Describe relapse warning signs you have concerns about, that were not on the previous list.

_____

_____

_____

_____

_____

_____

Pathway to an Addiction Free Lifestyle

_____
_____
_____
_____
_____
_____
_____
_____

Exercise # 5 — Step-down Relapse Prevention Packet

Identifying Critical Warning Signs

Critical warning signs are those that you can identify early and manage differently in order to avoid relapse.

1. Review the warning sign list provided on pages G14-G16, and those warning signs you described.

2. If you believe a warning sign is critical put a star (*) by it in the margin. Your goal is to identify all of your critical warning signs.

Review all of your critical warning signs and chose three that you believe to be the most critical. List these three most critical warning signs below and answer the question about these warning signs.

Critical Warning Sign #1: _____

Why I selected this warning sign: _____

_____

_____

Critical Warning Sign #2: _____

Why I selected this warning sign: _____

_____

Pathway to an *Addiction Free* Lifestyle

Critical Warning Sign #3: _____

Why I selected this warning sign: _____

_____

_____

Exercise # 6 — Step-down Relapse Prevention Packet

Managing Critical Warning Signs

Part A.

1. What is the first critical warning sign you selected?

_____

_____

_____

2. Describe your thoughts when this warning sign is activated.

_____

_____

_____

3. Describe your feelings when this warning sign is activated.

_____

_____

_____

4. Describe how this warning sign is exhibited in your actions.

_____

_____

Pathway to an *Addiction Free* Lifestyle

5. Describe what actions you have an urge to do when this warning sign is activated.

_____

_____

_____

6. Describe what healthy actions you can choose to take to cope with this warning sign.

_____

_____

_____

7. Describe what healthy thoughts you can choose to cope with this warning sign.

_____

_____

_____

8. Describe what feelings you are likely to have if you choose the above healthy actions and thoughts.

_____

_____

_____

Part B.

1. What is the second critical warning sign you selected?

_____

_____

_____

2. Describe your thoughts when this warning sign is activated.

Pathway to an *Addiction Free* Lifestyle

3. Describe your feelings when this warning sign is activated.

4. Describe how this warning sign is exhibited in your actions.

5. Describe what actions you have an urge to do when this warning sign is activated.

6. Describe what healthy actions you can choose to take to cope with this warning sign.

7. Describe what healthy thoughts you can choose to cope with this warning sign.

8. Describe what feelings you are likely to have if you choose the above healthy actions and thoughts.

Pathway to an *Addiction Free* Lifestyle

_____
_____
_____

Part C.

1. What is the third critical warning sign you selected?

_____
_____
_____

2. Describe your thoughts when this warning sign is activated.

_____
_____
_____

3. Describe your feelings when this warning sign is activated.

_____
_____
_____

4. Describe how this warning sign is exhibited in your actions.

_____
_____
_____

5. Describe what actions you have an urge to do when this warning sign is activated.

_____
_____

Pathway to an *Addiction Free* Lifestyle

6. Describe what healthy actions you can choose to take to cope with this warning sign.

_____

_____

_____

7. Describe what healthy thoughts you can choose to cope with this warning sign.

_____

_____

_____

8. Describe what feelings you are likely to have if you choose the above healthy actions and thoughts.

_____

_____

_____

Pathway to an *Addiction Free* Lifestyle

PERSONAL RECOVERY PLAN

DAILY RECOVERY PROGRAM

1. BEGIN EACH DAY WITH AN INSPIRATIONAL THOUGHT

2. READ MOTIVATIONAL LITERATURE EVERY DAY

3. GO TO A MEETING

4. TALK TO ANOTHER ADDICT/ALCOHOLIC

5. END EACH DAY WITH AN INSPIRATIONAL THOUGHT

6. _____

7. _____

8. _____

9. _____

10. _____

PERSONAL RELAPSE PREVENTION PLAN

1. <u>People</u> that could be harmful to my recovery:

_____

_____

_____

Actions I can do to protect my recovery in regard to these people:

_____

_____

_____

Pathway to an *Addiction Free* Lifestyle

Thoughts I can choose to protect my recovery in regard to these people:

_____

_____

_____

2. <u>Places</u> that could be harmful to my recovery:

_____

_____

_____

Actions I can take to protect my recovery in regard to these places:

_____

_____

_____

Thoughts I can choose to protect my recovery in regard to these places:

_____

_____

_____

3. <u>Things</u> that could be harmful to my recovery:

_____

_____

_____

Actions I can take to protect my recovery in regard to these things:

_____

_____

_____

Pathway to an *Addiction Free* Lifestyle

Thoughts I can choose to protect my recovery in regard to these things:

_____

_____

_____

4. <u>Situations</u> that could be harmful to my recovery:

_____

_____

_____

Actions I can take to protect my recovery in regard to these situations:

_____

_____

_____

Thoughts I can choose to protect my recovery in regard to these places:

_____

_____

_____

3. <u>Things</u> that could be harmful to my recovery:

_____

_____

_____

Actions I can to protect my recovery in regard to these things:

_____

_____

_____

Pathway to an *Addiction Free* Lifestyle

Thoughts I can choose to protect my recovery in regard to these things:

___

___

___

4. <u>Situations</u> that could be harmful to my recovery:

___

___

___

Actions I can to protect my recovery in regard to these situations:

___

___

___

Thoughts I can choose to protect my recovery in regard to these situations:

___

___

___

5. <u>Times</u> of the year when it could be hard for me to protect my recovery:

___

___

___

Actions I can take to protect my recovery during these times of the year:

___

___

Pathway to an *Addiction Free* Lifestyle

Thoughts I could choose to protect my recovery during these times of the year:

_____

_____

_____

My <u>relapse warning signs</u> are:

_____

_____

_____

Healthy actions I choose to take to cope with my relapse warning signs:

_____

_____

_____

Healthy thoughts I can choose to cope with my relapse warning signs:

_____

_____

_____

<u>Feelings</u> that could be harmful to my recovery:

_____

_____

_____

Healthy actions I can choose to cope with these feelings:

_____

_____

Pathway to an *Addiction Free* Lifestyle

Healthy thoughts I can choose to cope with these feelings:

_____

_____

_____

Feelings, that are, helpful to my recovery:

_____

_____

_____

Actions I can choose to help produce these feelings:

_____

_____

_____

Thoughts I can choose to help produce these feelings:

_____

_____

_____

Pathway to an *Addiction Free* Lifestyle

RECOVERY GOALS

1. Personal Goals:

_____

_____

_____

2. Occupational/Educational Goals:

_____

_____

_____

3. Family Goals:

_____

_____

_____

4. Support System Goals:

_____

_____

_____

5. Twelve Step Goals:

_____

_____

_____

Pathway to an *Addiction Free* Lifestyle

Pathway to an *Addiction Free* Lifestyle

PARTICIPANT'S HANDOUTS

Pathway to an *Addiction Free* Lifestyle

Pathway to an *Addiction Free* Lifestyle

PEER EDUCATION PROGRAM

Immune System

This information is not meant to replace the medical counsel of your doctor or individual consultation with a registered dietitian. This information is informational and may only be used in its entirety.

Pathway to an *Addiction Free* Lifestyle

IMMUNE SYSTEM

THE IMMUNE SYSTEM

OVERVIEW

Just as the human mind allows a person to develop a concept of intellectual self, the immune system provides a concept of biologic self. The function of the immune system is to defend the body against invaders. Microbes (germs or microorganisms), cancer cells, and transplanted tissues or organs are all interpreted by the immune system as invaders against which the body must defend.

Although the immune system is complex its basic strategy is simple: to recognize the enemy, mobilize forces, and attack. Understanding the anatomy and components of the immune system makes it possible to see how this strategy works.

Each of you will be asked to fully participate in class discussion, and that may mean leaving your comfort zone to do something you have not been comfortable with in the past.

OBJECTIVES

By the end of the class students will be able to:

- State the purpose of the immune system
- Name the body's defense systems
- Name the components of the Immune System
- Describe the function of the T-Lymphocytes
- Describe the function of the B-Lymphocytes
- Name the four phases of the immune Response

> **OBJECTIVES**
> ✓ Purpose of the immune system
> ✓ The body's defense systems
> ✓ Components of the immune system
> ✓ Function of T-Lymphocytes
> ✓ Function of B-Lymphocytes
> ✓ Four phases of the immune response

> **IMMUNE SYSTEM**
>
> What is the immune system?
>
> Your body's defense against invasion from germs.

The Purpose of the Immune System

WHAT CAUSES AN INFECTION?

Germs cause infections.

What are germs? Microorganisms or microbes (tiny living body not seen by the naked eye) that causes disease. However there are an infinite number of microbes that do not cause disease.

> **Cells**
>
> Centrally located nucleus surrounded by a semi fluid liquid containing water, mineral, proteins, carbohydrates and lipids.
> Within the nucleus is:
> Nucleic Acid
> Deoxyribonnucleic acid (DNA)
> Ribonucleic Acid (RNA)

Let's look at the good surrounding all of us in the come into contact with every discovery that every aspect of our natural world is affected for good or ill by the activities of tiny, unseen microbes (bacteria, viruses, fungi, and protozoa).

MICROBES

Helpful microbes enable us to:

- Leaven bread and make cheese and yogurt
- Ferment fine wines and beer
- Recycle our garbage and human remains back to the soil
- Digest our food and make vitamins
- Process sewage disposal into clean, safe, drinking water
- Produce antibiotics and other medicines

> **Helpful Microbes**
>
> ✓ Leaven bread, make cheese and yogurt
> ✓ Ferment wine and beer
> ✓ Digest our food and produce vitamins
> ✓ Process sewage disposal
> ✓ Produce antibiotics and other medicines

However, when the microbes are harmful to the host (whether human, animal, plants or microbes) they are called pathogens.

> **PATHOGENS**
>
> ✓ Microorganisms capable of producing disease

PATHOGENS

Pathogens are microorganisms capable of producing disease. Among these are **bloodborne** pathogens, which are responsible for the transmission of infectious diseases such as Human Immunodeficiency Virus (HIV) and Hepatitis. These are transmitted to another individual through exposure to blood, blood products, and bodily fluids, such as semen, vaginal secretions, tears, urine, and milk.

CELLS

Cells are the structural unit of plant and animal life. The cellular function is an essential process of living things. Cells arise only from pre-existing cells; new cells arise by cell division. Growth and development result in the increase in the numbers of cells and their specialization into different types of tissues, such as basal, or skin cells, blood, fat and giant cells which are found in the bone marrow.

CELLS
DNA
✓ Give rise to chromosome, the origin of our inherited characteristic, i.e. eye color, hair color, height.

Cells consist of a centrally located nucleus surrounded by a semi fluid liquid consisting of water, mineral, proteins, carbohydrates and lipids. Within the nucleus is nucleic acid, or deoxyribonucleic acid (DNA) or ribonucleic acid (RNA).

DNA contains chromosomes (the origin of our inherited characteristic, e.g. whether your hair is brown or red, or whether you are tall or short).

MICROORGANISMS

Bacteria
✓ Tiny creature
✓ Microscopic organism
✓ One celled
✓ Reproduce by simple division
✓ Most can be killed by antibiotics
✓ Like moist warm environments

Bacteria are tiny creatures, microscopic organisms; they are typically one celled and reproduce by simple division. Most can be killed with antibiotics.

They like warm, moist environments.

Viruses are extremely small germs that invade, damage, and kill cells. They are pathogens to all forms of life, humans, animals, plants, and even to bacteria. They are so small they can only be detected with the use of an electron microscope, and can cause the most virulent (or highly infectious) epidemics. A virus germ invades a cell, subtly changing the cell's natural functions. Once it is inside the cell, the cell is unable to continue to make healthy cells using its own DNA center. It must instead make copies of the virus using the virus DNA or RNA. As a result, the invaded cell is manufacturing more viral particles. This usually kills the cells, which breaks apart and releases thousands of virus copies into the blood. A virus can remain dormant (or inactive) in the host for months or years, then reactivate, even after treatment.

VIRUS
✓ Ultra microscopic
✓ Can only reproduce with living cells
✓ Lives in your body forever
✓ Invades cells and becomes part of cell's machinery
✓ Cells then produce copies of infected cells
✓ Consists of DNA/RNA within a protein case

Parasites are organisms, which live on an organism of another species from which it derives food or protection. You don't have to have sex to get infected by a parasite; they can be transmitted by close physical contact. Parasites can also live on clothing, towels, and sheets and sometimes even toilet seats.

> **PARASITES**
> - ✓ Lives on other organisms
> - ✓ Derives its food from other organisms.
> - ✓ Don't have to have sex to get infected
> - ✓ Transmitted by <u>CLOSE PHYSICAL CONTACT</u>
> - ✓ Can live on inanimate objects

> **FUNGI**
> - ✓ Grow in single cells or
> - ✓ Multi-cellular colonies
> - ✓ Obtain food from dead or living organic matter
> - ✓ Can cause death in an Immuno-compromised person.

Fungi grow in single cells, as in yeast, or multi-cellular colonies, such as molds and mushrooms. They do not contain chlorophyll, and they obtain food from dead or living organic matter. Most fungi are not pathogenic, and the body's normal flora contains many fungi. In immunocompetent humans overgrowth of fungi can cause minor infections of the hair, nails, mucous membranes, or skin. In a person with a compromised immune system due to HIV disease or immunosuppressive drug therapy, fungi are a source of opportunistic infections that can cause death. Fungi live on your skin and mucus membranes. A problem develops when there is an overgrowth of fungus. Growth can be triggered by stress, diet and transmitted by a sexual partner.

THE IMMUNE SYSTEM

In order to understand the complex interaction of the immune system: let's first discuss how the body resists infection.

Everyday about 7 billion people are exposed to countless types of bacteria, viruses and fungi. Without a method of protection against these and other health contaminants. human life would cease to exist, as we know it. If you ask the average person why they are healthy, they will probably give you a vague answer. Maybe they'll answer, "Because I eat healthy foods and exercise," or "because I take care of myself".

These answers may account for fitness and wellness in a person, but each has forgotten the key component of healthiness. Almost no one ever acknowledges the real defensive strength of our body, the human immune system. The immune system, although used as a collective term, is not one large organ that protects our bodies. In fact; the human immune system is a cooperation of different types of cells, tissues and enzymes. Each part of the immune system network has its own specialized tasks and, as a whole, this biological system is one of the most complex known to man. The main function of the immune system is to identify and eliminate all threatening foreign elements from our bodies. Nature has designed our defense system so well that the majority of free radicals, which enters our body, are immediately rejected.

DEFENSE BARRIERS

The first barriers of defense are known as nonspecific, meaning they are naturally in place to ward off any object or organism from entering the body.

Intact skin - The skin is the first line of defense against the transmission of most disease and prevents many foreign substances, such as splinters, from entering the body.

The skin is coated with oils and moisture from the sebaceous and sweat glands. These inhibit bacterial growth. The skin will cleanse itself of adherent microorganisms by steadily sloughing off the old skin and replacing it with new layers.

> **DEFENSE**
>
> Intact Skin
> ✓ First line against transmission of diseases and prevent foreign substances from entering the body
> ✓ Bathed in oil and moisture from sebaceous and sweat glands

> **DEFENSE**
>
> Mucous membranes
> ✓ Found in the eyes, nose and mouth it is equivalent to the skin
> ✓ A sticky fluid that entraps small foreign particles so they can be swept away or expelled through such actions as sneezing or coughing

Mucous membranes — Certain interior parts of the body are exposed to the outside environment though the eyes, mouth, and nose. These parts (in addition to the other linings of the digestive, respiratory, reproductive, and urinary tract) are lined with the equivalent of the skin called the mucous membrane. These membranes secrete a sticky fluid (mucus) that entraps small foreign particles so they can be swept away or expelled through such actions as coughing or sneezing.

Chemical barriers such as sweat, skin oils, tears, and stomach acid, are toxic to many types of bacteria. If microorganisms enter the body through the mouth and are swallowed, they'll encounter a hostile environment of hydrochloric acid in the stomach. Most bacteria are killed by this gastric activity.

Another chemical agent used by the body is found in tears (lysozyme). **Lysozyme** is an immune agent that breaks chemical bonds in the cell walls of bacteria and kills them.

> **DEFENSE**
>
> Chemical Barriers
> ✓ Sweat, skin oil, tears and stomach acid are toxic to many bacteria

> **DEFENSE**
> Inflammatory response
> ✓ Occurs when bacteria or foreign objects attack the exposed, nutrient-rich cells beneath the skin

The inflammatory response occurs when bacteria or exposed, nutrient-rich cells beneath the skin. This is the other front — inflammation — which is a tissue reaction to an injury or disease-causing agent. Inflammation is the body's way of responding to a localized attack. This is a nonspecific response triggered by bumps and blows, a prick on the finger, too much sun, burns, or frostbite, radiation, or corrosive acids and alkali. Bacteria and other microbes are not essential causes of inflammation, although they are common.

Inflammatory responses may include:

Redness — due to dilatation of blood vessels close to the surface of the skin since the area is immersed in blood

Swelling — due to release of blood plasma or fluid into the wound area

Heat — as a consequence of the infusion of warm plasma into the tissues

Pain — from the abundance of nerve ending that respond to the growing pressure caused by the congestion of blood and fluid

> **DEFENSE**
> **Inflammatory responses include:**
> ✓ **Redness** - Dilation of blood vessels
> ✓ **Swelling** - Release of fluid into the wounded area
> ✓ **Heat** - A consequence of the infusion of warm plasma into the tissue
> ✓ **Pain** - Nerve endings that respond to the growing pressure from congestion of blood and fluid

Inflammation is generally effective in restoring the (homeostasis). However, sometimes these side effects individual and temporarily may limit function.

The Immune Response — Finally, what is remarkable about how the body resists disease is what occurs should any invader penetrate the physical and chemical barriers of the body. If this occurs Special Forces will be summoned to complete the mission of saving your life. This is the immune response, which can take aim and target invaders with "pinpoint precision".

If an invader penetrates the physical and chemical barriers of the body, special forces will be summoned to complete the mission of saving your life.

This process is called:

The Immune Response

Imagine the immune system as a flowing highway of cells designed to respond to infections caused by foreign invaders. The highway is the **lymphatic system**, which filters unwanted material through nodes that run into large ducts and finally drain

> **DEFENSE**
> ✓ If an invader penetrates the physical and chemical barriers of the body, special forces will be summoned to complete the mission of saving your life.
> ✓ This process is called
>   The Immune Response

into the venous system (veins) throughout the body.

Traveling on the highway are lymphocytes. small white blood cells that include families of B and T cells. These cells get their name from their different paths of development. B cells are derived in bone marrow; T cells in the thymus gland.

The immune response will recognize invading organisms as antigens, which are proteins that differ from our normal body proteins. If viruses, for example, enter the body, they'll cleverly disguise themselves by hiding in host cells. Even so, the immune response is triggered and set into action.

Each immune response has four phases:

> **DEFENSE**
> **Four phases of the Immune Response:**
> ✓ Recognizing the enemy
> ✓ Mounting defenses
> ✓ Attack
> ✓ Suppression of immune response

1. Recognizing the enemy

2. Mounting defenses

3. Attack

4. Suppression of immune response (shutting off response when job is completed)

If the same enemy reappears in the body, the immune response is immediate. Both B and T cells to 'remember' particular invaders.

COMPONENTS OF THE IMMUNE SYSTEM

WHITE BLOOD CELLS

White blood cells are the primary fighting cells against infection and tissue damage. They not only neutralize or destroy organisms, but also act as scavengers, cleaning up damaged cells by phagocytosis (process of ingesting and digesting germs) to initiate the repair process.

> **COMPONENTS**
> - ✓ White blood cells – Phagocytosis
> - ✓ Thymus – Produces T-lymph cells
> - ✓ Spleen – Filters
> - ✓ Lymph System – Removes excreta from body
> - ✓ Bone Marrow – Produces B-lymph cells
> - ✓ Antibodies – kills invading germs
> - ✓ Complement system – produces protein

TYPES OF WHITE BLOOD CELLS

> **White Blood Cells**
> Granulocytes
> - ✓ Neutrophil – Destroys germs
> - ✓ Basophil – Secrets chemical
> - ✓ Eosinophil – May destroy parasites

Granulocytes

There are three types of granulocytes located in the immune system. The most common is called the Neutrophil. This cell makes up an average 58% of the white cells in the body. Neutrophils are attracted to the site of injury and infection where they stick to the blood vessel walls and overwhelm the bacteria or foreign body. The Eosinophils make up about 2% of the white cells and create the effects of allergic reaction and they defend against parasites. Basophils are about one percent of the white cells in the body. They contain histamines and other compounds, which help in the first stages of infections.

Monocytes

Monocytes are the largest of the white cells, and make up an average 4% of the white cells in the body. These cells usually leave the bloodstream and become macrophages, which go into the tissue. Their main function is to help to defend against fungi and diseases like Tuberculosis.

> **MONOCYTES**
> - ✓ Largest of the white cells
> - ✓ Develops into Macrophages that ingest and destroys germs
> - ✓ Defend against fungi and diseases such as TB
> - ✓ Inhabit more susceptible areas of the body, to protect vital organs

Although Monocytes are quite small they can transform into larger, more powerful cell called macrophages. Macrophages contain lysosomes full of special enzymes and chemicals, which allow them to ingest and digest dangerous microbes. These cells do not circulate in the blood stream. Macrophages inhabit the more susceptible areas of the body, to protect the body's vital organs.

LYMPHOCYTES

> **Lymphocytes**
> - Created in the bone marrow
> - Cells that leave and matures in the Thymus and called T-cells
> - Cells that stay and mature in the bone marrow are called B-cells

Lymphocytes are cells present in the blood and the lymphatic tissue. Less than 4% is present in the circulating blood. These cells travel from the blood to the lymph nodes and lymph nodes and back into the circulation. There are a number of different types of lymphocytes with respect to function. They are derived from the stem cells from which all blood cells arise.

They are the main means of providing the body with immune capability. This is done by means of humoral immunity (antibody production) produced by the B cells (produced in the bone marrow) and cell-mediated immunity produced by T cells (produced by the thymus gland).

B-Lymphocytes

B-Lymphocytes are produced in the bone marrow. These white blood cells are responsible for the production of antibodies (also called immunoglobulins). There are five types of immunoglobulins (abbreviated ig): IgG, IgM, IgE, IgA and IgD. These are Y-shaped molecules that have a variable segment that is a binding site for only one specific antigen. Some B-lymphocytes stay in the body as "memory cells" so that if a particular virus or bacteria enters the body again they will quickly produce antibodies to destroy it.

> **White Blood Cells**
> Lymphocytes
> - B-Lymphocytes – memory cells, produce antibodies
> - T-Lymphocytes – T4 – T8 – Suppressor cells, help protect against viral infection

T-Lymphocytes

T-Lymphocytes, which account for 75% of lymphocytes, are produced in the thymus gland. These white blood cells are responsible for the coordination of the immune response. The T cell family includes the T-helper (CD4), T-killer (CD8), and T-suppresser cells.

CD4 CELLS

> **The T-Cell Battle**
> - T.-helper (CD4), sounds the alarm and activates antibody production
> - T-killer (CD8), multiply and attack invader
> - T-suppresser, calls off attack after battle is won

One of the immune system's most important players is the CD4 cell (T-helper). The T-helper sounds the alarm (by releasing substances) that activates antibody production. Killer T cells are also beckoned to multiply and attack. The killer T cells then begin shooting holes in host cells that have been infected by viruses. If they survive, they will continue to kill more of the enemy. When the battle is won, the T-suppresser cells call off the attack.

On the battlefield, the effectiveness of the immune response relies on CD4s (T-helpers) to initiate an attack on antigens. This is why HIV is so alarming. The virus attacks the protective leaders of the immune response and turns them into HIV factories. As HIV copies are manufactured, the CD4 cells are effectively destroyed over time.

HIV attacks both "activated" CD4 cells, which have been "turned on" and are dividing and actively fighting infection as well as "resting" CD4 cells, which have not encountered any infection and are waiting to be called into action.

THYMUS

The thymus is important in the development of the immune response in newborns. It is essential to the maturation of the lymphoid T cells.

> **THYMUS**
> ✓ Important in the development of immune response in newborns
> ✓ Essential for the production of T-lymphocytes

SPLEEN

Produces, monitors, stores, and destroys blood cells

Functions as two organs
- White pulp produces lymphocytes
- Red pulp removes unwanted material, (i.e. bacteria & defective red blood cells)

> **SPLEEN**
> ✓ Produces, monitors, stores and destroys blood cells
> ✓ Functions as two organs:
>   - White pulp produces lymphocytes
>   - Red pump removes unwanted material, i.e., bacteria and defective red blood cells.

LYMPH SYSTEM

The lymphatic system is a network of lymph nodes connected by lymphatic vessels. Lymph nodes contain a mesh of tissues which lymphocytes are tightly packed. This mesh of lymphocytes filters, attacks, and destroys harmful organisms that cause infections. Lymph nodes are often clustered in areas where the lymphatic vessels branch off, such as the neck, armpits, and groin.

> **Lymphatic System**
> ✓ Network of lymph nodes
> ✓ Lymphatic vessels
> ✓ Lymph fluid (rich in white blood cells)

Lymph, a fluid rich in white blood cells, flows through the lymphatic vessels. Lymph helps return water, proteins, and other substances from the body' tissues to the bloodstream. All substances absorbed by the lymph pass through at least one lymph node and its filtering mesh of lymphocytes.

BONE MARROW

Bone Marrow
- ✓ Produces new blood cells, both red and white
- ✓ Red blood cells fully form in the marrow
- ✓ White cells usually mature elsewhere
- ✓ Stem cells

Bone marrow produces new blood cells, both red and white. In the case of red blood cells, the cells are fully formed in the marrow and then they enter the blood stream. In the case of some white blood cells, the cells mature elsewhere. The marrow produces all blood cells from stem cells. They are called "stem cells" because they can branch off and become many different types of cells. Stem cells change into actual, specific types of white blood cells.

ANTIBODIES

Complex protein produced by the B-lymphocytes in response to the presence of antigens. Antibodies neutralize or destroy antigens in several ways. They can initiate lysis (the gradual decline of the disease process) of the antigen by activating the complement system, neutralizing toxins released by bacteria, opsonizing the antigen or forming a complex to stimulate phagocytosis, promoting antigen clumping (agglutination), or preventing the antigen from adhering to host cells.

ANTIBODIES
- ✓ Immunogobulins are produced by white blood cells (Y-shaped proteins that respond to a specific Antigen)
- ✓ Antibodies bind to the outer coat of a virus particle or the cell wall of a bacterium and stop its movement through cell walls
- ✓ Complements "coat" the invader so it can be "recognized" by white cells

COMPLEMENT SYSTEM
- ✓ Like antibodies the complement system is a series of proteins
- ✓ There are millions of different antibodies in the blood stream each sensitive to a specific antigen
- ✓ There is only a handful of protein in the complement system and are floating freely in your blood, but inactive
- ✓ Complements are manufactured in the liver and activated by and work with the antibodies
- ✓ They cause lysing (bursting) of cells and signals to phagocytes that a cell needs to be removed

COMPLEMENT SYSTEM

The complement system is a group of proteins in the blood that play a vital role in the body's immune defenses through a cascade of interactions. Complements act by directly lysing (killing) organisms; by opsonizing (coating an antigen with a substance making them more susceptible to macrophages) an antigen, thus stimulating phagocytosis; and by stimulating inflammation and the B cell mediated immune response.

FIGHTING OFF AN INFECTION

1. It all starts with a breech in our security system. A virus can enter our bodies through any break in the skin or opening at all. Some viruses can be contracted orally, some through cuts, scrapes, and some through sexual intercourse. Usually any exchanging of bodily fluids will do it. Once the virus is inside our body, the action begins.

   RESPONSE
   - ✓ Phagocyte cells – Neutrophil and Macrophage begin to ingest the foreign particle
   - ✓ Chemicals are released into the system that calls the T-4 cells
   - ✓ The T-4 cells summons the T-8 cells, these are called Killer cells

2. The immune system begins its response when a white blood cell, usually a macrophage, comes in contact with a virus and devours it. Of course, this doesn't stop all the other infecting viruses from spreading throughout the host's cells. Our immune system usually comes into play after the viruses have already done most of their infecting.

3. After the macrophage gets a good taste of the virus, it gives up little pieces of the virus, which are displayed on its outer shell. These little virus samples are called antigens. These antigens act as homing beacons for leukocytes. Basophils are also created, and they begin to release histamines. From here inflammation is initiated as the first steps towards overcoming the infection.

4. Now specialized helper T cells identify the antigens and form a union with the macrophage. This new partnership stimulates the creation of lots of different chemicals, such as cytokine, all of which help establish intercellular communication to help mobilize the cells for the fight. It takes awhile for the body to produce the killer T cells specifically designed to target the virus. Hence the reason most people take seven to ten days to recover from the flu.

   RESPONSE
   - ✓ Once these cells have the attack under control the T-4 cells calls for the T-suppressor cells.
   - ✓ These cells suppress the T-8 cells so that the B-cells can finish the attack by producing an antibody for that specific antigen
   - ✓ The system then goes back to normal.

5. At this point helper T's and killer T's are rolling off the assembly line by the dozen. Chemical signals also cause an increase in the production of phagocytes. As all of this is happening, the matured helper T's are releasing chemicals which in turn signal B cells to multiply and start to manufacture antibodies. Finally the body's soldiers are trained and ready to go.

6. Now, the newly formed killer T cells begin their retaliation by puncturing the already infected host cells. The B cells then release antibodies, which bind to the viruses inside. This system destroys some of the lethal invaders and makes others more susceptible to attack from the phagocytes.

7. With antibodies helping to suppress the viruses, the macrophages are able to destroy viruses more easily. They are soon able to bring the infection under control. Monocytes help to clean up the mess of dead viruses and cells left behind from the attack, forming the yellow substance most of us call pus. All active T and B cells are suppressed and turned off by suppressor T cells.

8. The infection is now completely flushed from the system. Only memory cells remain behind, to keep the body on guard if the same virus attacks again.

DOCKING PROCEDURE

The question commonly asked is how does the virus attack and enter the T 4 cell? To answer this question we refer to the docking procedure. There are three steps in the docking procedures; the first and most critical of these is the viral entry.

Step I: Viral Entry

In order to replicate itself, an HIV particle must get its RNA, which is the genetic blueprint for a new particle, inside the host cell. To do that, the viral particle must first bind to two chief receptors on the host cell, much like a key fitting into a lock. If even one of those receptors, which are known as CD4 and CCR5 receptors, is missing, the viral core containing the RNA will not get into the cell. (Researchers have found that some AIDS patients, known as long-term non-progressors because they are HIV-positive yet show few or no symptoms of the disease, are missing the gene for one of these receptors.) The binding process is facilitated by a molecule on the surface of the HIV particle called gp120 (for glycoprotein with a molecular weight of 120). Once the viral particle has successfully bonded to the host cell, its core can pass through the cell wall into the cell's cytoplasm. The core then dissolves, leaving the RNA and catalyzing enzymes ready to begin the process of replication.

Step II: Viral Gene Transfer

Once inside the host cell, the viral RNA migrates toward the nucleus through the cell's cytoplasm and eventually through the nuclear membrane. A series of steps that ultimately ends in a new HIV particle. First, through a process known as reverse transcriptase catalyzes the formation of double-stranded viral DNA using the single-stranded viral RNA as a template. Employing other enzymes such as integrase, the new viral DNA then breaks open the host cell's DNA and integrates itself into it. This leads to the formation of a new viral RNA strand, which migrates out of the host's DNA. The new viral RNA moves into the cytoplasm, where new viral proteins are built using the viral RNA as a blueprint.

Step III: Viral Exit

Once the viral protein parts have been built, they are assembled into a new HIV particle. This particle is an exact duplicate of the HIV particle from which it sprung, complete with two copies of viral RNA and the enzymes needed for reverse transcription. The new HIV particle moves out of the cell, where it heads off to infect another cell and perpetuate the life cycle.

This process repeats itself continuously, with many millions of HIV particles produced simultaneously in the body. After repeated assaults by viral particles, the host cell dies, having exhausted their energy and molecular building supplies while generating HIV viruses. This suppresses a patient's immune system and leaves him open to infection by other infectious agents, including bacteria, fungi, and other viruses.

CONCLUSION

The immune system is a very fascinating system that has many different functions. Like a well-oiled machine the immune system protects the body against the invasion of pathogens that are determined to destroy or break it down. The body's line of defense when intact, protects it from many pathogen that try to destroy it daily, when this system is down the immune response takes over.

OBJECTIVES

We have discussed in detail the following:

- The purpose of the immune system
- The body's defense systems
- The components of the Immune System
- The function of the T-Lymphocytes
- The function of the B-Lymphocytes
- The four phases of the Immune Response

Pathway to an *Addiction Free* Lifestyle

Immune System

1) The purpose of the immune system as discussed in the lesson plan is to:

   A. Complex system to recognize invaders

   B. Defend the body against invaders

   C. A concept of biologic self

   D. All of the above

2) Most bacteria can be killed with antibiotics

   A. True

   B. False

3) Components of the immune system discussed:

   A. White blood cells

   B. Lymphocytes

   C. Thymus

   D. All of the above

4) Function of the T-Lymphocytes against viruses:

   A. Cells that attack host cells that have a virus

   B. Anatomical Body Fluid Test

   C. Western Blot

   D. Elisa Test

5) The function of the B-Lymphocytes in the Immune Response:

   A. Vitamin B replacement

   B. Not the means of providing the body with immune capabilities

   C. Production of antibodies

6) Four phases of the Immune Response

A. Recognizing the enemy

B. Mounting defenses

C. Attack

D. Suppression of immune response

E. All of the above

7) The skin is the first line of defense against infection

A. True

B. False

8) What can cause the skin defense to break down?

A. A tear in the skin

B. Hugging an infected person

C. Breathing in a closed room with infected person

9) The immune response can take aim and target invader with "pinpoint precision"

A. True

B. False

10) Natural defenses of the body against illness or disease?

A. Tears

B. Skin

C. Sever night sweats

D. A and B above

Answers:

(1) D (2) A (3) D (4) A (5) C (6) E (7) A (8) A (9) A (10) D

Pathway to an *Addiction Free* Lifestyle

PEER EDUCATION PROGRAM

HEPATITIS

This information is not meant to replace the medical counsel of your doctor or' individual consultation with a registered dietitian. This information is informational and may only be used in its entirety.

Pathway to an *Addiction Free* Lifestyle

Pathway to an Addiction Free Lifestyle

The ABC's of Viral Hepatitis

OVERVIEW

Many of us go through life never having a problem with our liver; as a result of this we never know the importance of this organ. That can be a good thing or a bad thing. Did you know that there are over 200 functions associated with the liver? These functions allow us to maintain our daily living routines. The things we take for granted such as digesting our foods, cleaning toxin from the body or just boosting our immune system, are important functions of the liver. It is clear that the body could not stay on task without the liver. To keep the liver healthy we must learn to take care of this vital organ. In this lesson, we will discuss the proper care for the liver. This includes nutrition and using universal precautions. During this class, we will talk about what happens if the liver becomes diseased or infected. We will discuss the organisms that cause these infections and how they spread from person to person. There is a serious health concern in our institutions today.

ABC's OF HEPATITIS
The Time to Get the Facts is Now

What is the liver?
✓ It is the 'largest internal organ'
✓ The 'all chemical wizard'

That concern is hepatitis, (inflammation of the liver). This disease is a problem in our prison system, because of certain risky behaviors that allows the disease to be spread from person to person. We will talk about ways to limit that transmission.

OBJECTIVES

By the end of this course, you will be able to:

- Identify the viral strains of hepatitis discussed in the lesson.

- Name the functions of the liver discussed in the lesson.

- Discuss the different transmission routes for each of the viral strains of Hepatitis.

OBJECTIVES
✓ Identify the viral stains of Hepatitis
✓ Name the functions of the liver
✓ Identify the transmission routes of each of the viral strains of Hepatitis

HOW THE LIVER FUNCTIONS

The liver is the largest organ in your body, about the size of a football in an adult. It is tucked up under the ribs on the right side of your body. The primary functions of the liver are digestive and metabolic. This organ refines and detoxifies everything you eat, breathe, and absorb through your skin. It is your body's internal chemical power plant, converting nutrients in the food you eat into muscles, energy, hormones, clotting factors, and immune factors.

LIVER
- ✓ Largest organ in the body
- ✓ Size of a football
- ✓ Located on right side
- ✓ Over 200 functions

You cannot hear or feel your liver. You will not know it is there unless you are very sick because the liver is a non-complaining organ. However, when liver cells become permanently damaged or scarred from drinking too much alcohol, ingesting drugs, or by disease, a condition known as cirrhosis occurs. Conditions that damage the liver are: Fibrosis — is a condition where the good tissues of the liver are replaced by damaged tissue. This condition leads to cirrhosis. Cirrhosis — is a permanent scarring of the liver that may result from any of the causes of hepatitis. Alcohol and viral hepatitis are responsible for at least 95% of the cases of cirrhosis in the U.S. Liver failure - is a condition where the liver has ceased to perform most of its common functions causing the body to not function normally. Liver cancer — is a malignancy of the liver that results from the spread of a primary source or from a primary tumor of the liver itself. Chronic hepatitis B is a risk factor for primary liver cancer.

Liver Damage
- ✓ Fibrosis – Damaged tissue
- ✓ Cirrhosis – Scarred liver from chronic inflammation
- ✓ Liver Failure – Liver is not functioning properly
- ✓ Liver Cancer – Chronis Hepatitis B and C are a risk for liver cancer

There have been more than 200 functions attributed to the liver. Some of the primary liver functions include the following:

- Converts food into energy and stores it in liver cells (like a battery until you need it).

- Produces a digestive liquid called bile (the green liquid that tastes bad when you vomit) to help you absorb your vitamins and other nutrients. (Without the liver you would have vitamin deficiencies, fragile bones, and other problems.)

- Produces protein necessary to build your muscles (or else you would be weak).

- Stops cuts from bleeding by making clotting factors: a sticky substance like glue (or else you would bleed to death).

- Removes poisonous waste products from blood, and excretes or converts them into safer substances, e.g., toxins, fumes from paint thinners, bug and aerosol sprays, and poisonous chemicals in polluted air. (Tiny blood vessels in your lungs carry the toxins to your liver where they are detoxified and discharged into the bile.)

- Helps to create immune factors that protect you from germs and viruses that surround you.

Pathway to an Addiction Free Lifestyle

PROTECTING YOUR LIVER

- Eat a well-balanced diet.

- Wear a mask when working around exposure to fumes, toxins and poisonous chemicals.

- Drink alcohol in moderation.

- Do not take illegal drugs and take prescribed medication properly.

- Wash hands frequently to avoid germs, especially after using the toilet.

- Avoid sharing instruments contaminated with another's blood or body fluids.

> **Protecting Your Liver**
> ✓ Eat a well-balanced diet
> ✓ Mask up when working around poisonous chemicals
> ✓ Consume alcohol in moderation
> ✓ Wash hands
> ✓ Do not share personal hygiene

Some of the non-infectious causes include drinking too much alcohol, reactions to both legal and illegal drugs, and exposure to toxins in the environment. Viral hepatitis, however, is caused by one of the many hepatitis viruses.

> **What is Hepatitis?**
>
> Inflammation of the liver

TYPES OF HEPATITIS

Non-infectious hepatitis cannot be transmitted from person to person. It is usually acquired from chemicals, drugs, alcohol, and fumes that are in the environment.

Infectious hepatitis is usually caused by a virus (viral hepatitis) and can be spread from person to person by some vector. This form of hepatitis is broken down into two categories, acute (lasting less than six months) and chronic (lasting longer than six months). Certain forms of hepatitis will only be acute others will be acute and chronic.

> **What is Hepatitis?**
>
> Two Types of Hepatitis   Viral Strains
> - Viral or infectious   HAV   HDV
> - Non-Viral or Noninfectious HBV   HEV
>   HCV   HGV

TRANSMISSION ROUTES

Viral hepatitis is known as the alphabet virus, because there are five well-known kinds of hepatitis viruses currently identified as types A, B, C, D, and E in the United States. Other strains of Hepatitis include Type F (not confirmed yet) and Hepatitis G.

> **Transmission**
> Hepatitis A & E
> - Fecal oral route
> - Sexual practices
> - Contaminated food and water

While the transmission routes and treatment for viral hepatitis are distinct, the symptoms often appear indistinguishable. Another similarity is their target organ damage (since these viruses all replicate primarily in the liver). As we have said before, **viral hepatitis is an infectious cause for inflammation of the liver.** The hepatitis viruses differ in how they are transmitted, as well as how long and how severely they can affect you.

It is easier to be exposed to Hepatitis A (HAV) and E (HEV), which are primarily spread by the fecal-oral route, usually through anal-oral sexual contact ('rimming') or through contaminated food or water. This means the virus is spread by putting something in your mouth that is contaminated with infected feces (stool), or infected feces are contaminating the local water supplies. As the name implies, this form of hepatitis is contagious and is the cause of outbreaks, especially where sanitation is poor. Diaper changing tables, if not cleaned properly or the covering changed after each use may facilitate the spread of HAV or HEV.

> **Transmission**
> Hepatitis B, C, D & G
> Exposure to:
> - Blood
> - Blood products
> - Bodily fluids (semen, vaginal)

However, A, E, and G are milder forms compared to the other viral-strains, unless the individual is immunocompromised or co-infected with another hepatitis virus.

By comparison, bloodborne virus strains that cause the more serious types of infection are Hepatitis B (HBV), C (HCV), and D (HDV). These viruses are transmitted by exposure to the blood or body fluids of an infected person or having sex with an infected person can transmit HBV. Sexual transmission can also occur in a very small percentage of other hepatic viruses. Therefore, infection occurs similarly as the HIV virus that causes AIDS (Acquired Immune Deficiency Syndrome). Infants become infected by exposure to an infected mother's blood during birth. Hepatitis B and C can also be passed through exposure to sharp instruments contaminated with infected blood, such as tattooing, body piercing, and acupuncture needles, sharing razors or toothbrushes with an infected person, or human bites and through blood given before hepatitis testing was available.

SYMPTOMS OF VIRAL HEPATITIS

Hepatitis symptoms vary widely in severity. More importantly, many patients are asymptomatic, meaning they do not display any noticeable symptoms. Since the liver is a non-complaining organ, it is possible for individuals to be infected for years before they discover they are seriously ill. The hepatitis viruses are not transmitted the same way, but they can produce similar symptoms, such as:

- Fatigue
- Loss of appetite
- Mild fever and flu-like symptoms
- Muscle and joint aches
- Nausea and vomiting
- Diarrhea and abdominal discomfort
- Color changes in the urine (dark) and stool (clay-colored), a yellowing of the eyes and skin (jaundice)

Symptoms
- ✓ Fatigue
- ✓ Loss of appetite
- ✓ Mild Fever & flu-like symptoms
- ✓ Muscle & joint aches
- ✓ Nausea & vomiting
- ✓ Diarrhea, abdominal discomfort
- ✓ Color changes in the urine (dark) and stool (clay-colored)
- ✓ A yellowing of the eyes and skin (jaundice)

HEPATITIS A VIRUS (HAV)

Hepatitis A is the most common form of hepatitis with 29.1 - 33.5% of all Americans having been infected. Although, the number of cases continues to decrease in the U.S., there is still approximately 22,000 new infections each year according to the Center for Diseases Control and Prevention. The fecal-oral route, usually through person-to-person contact, or through contaminated food or water primarily spreads this strain. Diaper changing tables, if not cleaned properly or the covering changed after each use, may facilitate the spread of HAV.

If the contaminated feces somehow get on food, e.g., if an infected food handler handles food in a restaurant, the disease can spread quickly. Common source outbreaks have been related to food handlers who pass the virus on by not washing their hands with soap and water after having a bowel movement. Fruits, vegetables, sandwiches, or other uncooked foods can be contaminated with HAV during handling and spread the disease. Also, field crops picked by infected farm workers can contaminated. Other sources of infection include the following:

- Raw and undercooked shellfish harvested from contaminated waters.

- HAV is often seen in institutions for the mentally ill, convalescent homes, schools for retarded children, and daycare centers. It happens when there is either contact with feces during the changing of diapers or infected clothing.

- Anal-oral contact during sexual activity can lead to transmission.

- Persons who travel to areas where there is a high incidence of Hepatitis A. These areas inch_ de, but are not limited to, Africa, Asia (except Japan), the Mediterranean basin, Eastern Europe. the Middle East, Central and South America, Mexico, and parts of the Caribbean.

HAV is also spread within households. if a person is infected. Vaccination for household members with immune globulin is recommended.

When a person already infected with the Hepatitis C virus catches HAV, it may be rapidly fatal.

HEPATITIS B VIRUS (HBV)

Hepatitis B is one of the most prolific infectious diseases of our time, striking an estimated 4.3 5.6% of Americans. (According to the Centers for Disease Control and Prevention, in the U.S. an estimated 38,000 people contract the virus each year.) Approximately 90-95% of adults will recover within six months and not contact HBV again. However, blood tests will always show that they have been infected with HBV and the blood bank will not accept their blood.

Hepatitis B
- ✓ 38,000 Americans yearly
- ✓ 1.4 million with chronic infection

Hepatitis B
- ✓ Can unknowingly infect others
- ✓ 100 times more infectious than HIV
- ✓ Can remain undetected for years

HBV is a serious disease because this virus attacks the liver and, in a certain number of persons, can cause **lifelong infection**. As a result, up to 10 percent of adults; and 25 to 90 percent of children under the age of five, can develop acute and chronic liver diseases, such as cirrhosis and liver cancer (about 800,000 - 1.4 million people have chronic infection, and 3.000 people die from chronic liver disease associated with HBV each year).

Individuals with chronic HBV

Can unknowingly infect HEPATITIS B others.

Can unknowingly infect others

100 times more infectious than HIV

Individuals need to avoid body fluids, such as blood, semen, and vaginal secretions. HBV is primarily transmitted through unprotected sex, which accounts for more than 50 percent of acute HBV cases. It can also be passed through exposure to sharp instruments contaminated with infected blood, such as tattooing, body piercing, and acupuncture needles, sharing of razors or toothbrushes with an infected person, or human bites and through blood given before hepatitis B testing was available. HBV is at least

100 times more infectious than HIV. Perhaps the most striking feature of this disease is the ability to remain undetected for many years (those who display symptoms can mistake it for the flu).

HEPATITIS C VIRUS (HCV)

Hepatitis C
- ✓ 18,000 Americans are infected each year
- ✓ 3.9 million Americans are chronic carriers
- ✓ 50-80% of IDU become positive within 6-12 months of using
- ✓ IDU accounts for 50% of new infections

Hepatitis C was formerly known as post-transfusion, non-A, non-B hepatitis. Hepatitis C is a liver disease caused by the hepatitis C virus (HCV), which is found in the blood of persons who have this disease. HCV is spread by contact with the blood of an infected person. Although it was finally discovered in the early 1970's, a test for specific antibodies to the virus was not available until 1989. Prior to the identification of HCV, the majority of non-A, non-B hepatitis cases were associated with blood transfusions. Today, HCV is rarely transmitted by blood transfusion because of screening tests. There are several blood tests that can be done to determine if you have been infected with HCV. Your doctor may order just one or a combination of these tests. The following are types of tests your doctor may order and the purpose for each test:

- Anti-HCV (antibody to HCV) test for the presence of the virus.

- Qualitative tests to detect presence or absence of virus (HCV RNA).

- Quantitative tests to detect amount (titer) of virus (HCV RNA).

Still, the large reservoir of individuals already infected with HCV globally provide a source of transmission to others at risk, i.e., injection drug users (IDU). Each year, according to the Center for Disease Control and Prevention, about 18,000 Americans contract HCV and approximately 2.7 - 3.9 million people are chronic carriers, Hepatitis C is a more frequent cause of chronic liver disease than Hepatitis B (with 12,000 annual deaths from HCV). In drug users, HCV infection is acquired rapidly after beginning IDU, with 50 to 80 percent of new users becoming positive for HCV antibody within six-to-twelve months. Half of all infections annually are attributed to IDUs. HCV is spread primarily by direct contact with human blood. For example, you may have been infected with HCV if:

- You ever injected street drugs, as the needles and/or other drug "works" used to prepare or inject the drug(s) may have had someone else's blood that contained HCV on them.

- You received blood, blood products, or solid organs from a donor whose blood contained HCV.

- You were ever a healthcare worker and had frequent contact with blood on the job, especially accidental needle sticks.

- Your mother had hepatitis C at the time she gave birth to you. During birth her blood may have gotten into your body.

- You ever had sex with a person infected with HCV.

- You lived with someone who was infected with HCV and shared items such as razors or toothbrushes that might have had his/her blood on them.

Heptatis D
- ✓ Frequently causes chronic hepatitis
- ✓ Co-infection
- ✓ Super infection

HEPATITIS D VIRUS (HDV) ("Delta Virus")

HDV is a defective single-stranded RNA virus that requires the helper function of HBV to replicate. HDV requires HBV for synthesis of envelope protein composed of HBsAg, which is used to encapsulate the HDV genome. This is an extremely debilitating form of hepatitis which frequently causes chronic hepatitis. HDV infection can be acquired either as a co-infection with HBV or as a super-infection of persons with chronic HBV infection. Persons with HBV-HDV co-infection may have more severe acute disease and a higher risk of fulminant (having a rapid or severe onset) hepatitis (2%-20%) compared those infected with HBV alone; however, chronic HBV infection appears to occur less frequently in persons with HBV-HDV co-infection. Chronic HBV carriers who acquire HDV super-infection usually develop chronic HDV infection. In long-term studies of chronic HBV carriers with HDV super-infection,

70%-80% have developed evidence of chronic liver diseases with cirrhosis compared with 15%-30% of patients with chronic HBV infection alone.

HEPATITIS E VIRUS (HEV)

HEV is similar to Hepatitis A, in that they are both infectious and transmitted through the fecal-oral route. HEV occurs in epidemics in developing countries where there is fecal-contaminated water. It is rare in the United States. Usually HEV is not fatal, and there is no evidence of a chronic form. However, the exception is among pregnant women whose fatality rate can reach 20 percent if infected during the third trimester of pregnancy.

Hepatitis E
- ✓ Spread by fecal-oral
- ✓ Not common in USA
- ✓ No evidence of chronic form
- ✓ Dangerous to pregnant women

HEPATITIS G VIRUS (HGV)

Hepatitis G is a newly discovered form of liver inflammation caused by hepatitis G virus (HGV), a distant relative of the hepatitis C virus.

HEPATITIS G
- ✓ Blood born virus
- ✓ Little is known
- ✓ Often infected with HBV or HCV

HGV, also called hepatitis GB virus, was first described early in 1996. Little is known about the frequency of HGV infection, the nature of the illness, or how to prevent it. What is known is that transfused blood containing HGV has caused some cases of hepatitis. For this reason, patients with hemophilia and other bleeding conditions who require large amounts of blood or blood products are at risk of hepatitis G. HGV has been identified in between 1 - 2% of blood donors in the United States. Also at risk are patients with kidney disease who have blood exchange by hemodialysis, and those who inject drugs into their veins. It is possible that an infected mother can pass on the virus to their newborn infant. Sexual transmission is also a possibility.

Often patients with hepatitis G are infected at the same time by the hepatitis B or C virus, or both. In about three of every thousand patients with acute viral hepatitis, HGV is the only virus present. There is some indication that patients with hepatitis G may continue to carry the virus in their blood for many years, and so might be a source of infection in others.

RISK GROUPS OF VIRAL HEPATITIS

Anyone who is exposed to blood, semen, and vaginal secretions is at risk for hepatitis. Individuals considered at high risk include the following:

- Recipients of blood products
- Injection drug users
- Tattoo and skin piercing
- Sexually active homosexual and bisexual men who do not practice safer sex (e.g., the use of condoms)
- Anyone having unsafe sex with a chronic hepatitis carrier
- Persons in occupations that have contact with blood
- Hemophiliacs and hemodialysis patients
- Babies born to infected mothers
- Prisoners and others in long-term facilities
- Travelers to developing countries
- Household members of those with HAV and HBV

Who's At Risk
- ✓ Recipients of blood & blood products
- ✓ Injection drug users, tattoos & skin piercing
- ✓ Sexually active homosexual & bisexual men who do not practice safe sex
- ✓ Anyone having sex with a chronic hepatitis carrier
- ✓ Occupations that have contact with blood
- ✓ Babies born to infected mothers
- ✓ Prisoners & others in long-term facilities
- ✓ Travelers to developing countries
- ✓ Household members of those infected with HAV & HB

PREVENTION OF VIRAL HEPATITIS

To prevent viral hepatitis infection, you need to:

- Get vaccinated
- Practice safer sex
- Wash hands after going to the bathroom
- Not share needles, or use illegal IV drugs
- Avoid tattoos and body piercing. Both needles and ink are particularly when used by nonprofessionals
- Use precautions when handling blood or blood spills
- Handle razors, knives, and other sharp instruments with care
- Not share toothbrushes or any other object, which may come into contact with blood or body fluids.

> **Prevention**
> ✓ Get vaccinated
> ✓ Practice safer sex
> ✓ Wash hands
> ✓ Do not share needles or use illegal drugs
> ✓ Avoid tattoos and body piercing
> ✓ Use universal precautions
> ✓ Handle 'sharps' with care
> ✓ Do not share objects which may come into contact with blood or bodily fluids

Prevention, prevention, prevention is the first line of defense against viral hepatitis. Once infected, medical treatment has only varying success.

TREATMENT FOR VIRAL HEPATITIS

The Centers for Disease Control and Prevention recommends that certain individuals get vaccinated for Hepatitis A and B.

> **Treatment**
> Get vaccinated for HAV & HBV

A vaccine is an inactive part of a virus or a similar non-harmful virus, given to a healthy person. It promotes a mock infection of a disease. This will trigger the immune system to build antibodies to fight it. If exposed to the actual virus later, the body can produce more rapidly the antibodies it needs to defend itself. For example, for many years, individuals were vaccinated against the deadly smallpox virus with an inactivated cowpox virus.

Immune globulins (called "IG's") are an important tool for preventing viral infections. They can also stop the progression of disease if administered shortly after exposure. The IG's that are used in medical practice are sterile solutions of antibodies (immunoglobulins) derived from human plasma.

Only plasma shown to be free of blood borne pathogens, such as viral hepatitis and HIV is used to prepare IG's. These vaccines are safe and effective, and provide protection from infection. At present, there are no vaccines for Hepatitis C, D. or E.

HEPATITIS CARRIER

Individuals who cannot clear the virus from their blood within six months are considered to be chronically infected and are called hepatitis carriers. Individuals with long-term infection usually have no signs or symptoms, and can unknowingly pass the virus to others. Hepatitis carriers need to take extra precautions for themselves and to prevent infecting others. They need to:

> **Hepatitis Carrier**
> ✓ Regular monitoring
> ✓ Talk to sex partner
> ✓ Be careful with medications
> ✓ Avoid alcohol
> ✓ Tell doctors & Dentists your status
> ✓ Cover all cuts
> ✓ Wipe up blood spills
> ✓ Stop sharing toothbrushes, razors, needles, syringes, nail files, clippers
> ✓ Stop donating blood, plasma, body organs, tissue or sperm

- Have regular monitoring (at least once a year) of their liver to determine if the disease is progressing; and, periodic tests for liver cancer.

- Tell sexual partners they are a "carrier", practice safer sex; and have partners vaccinated.

- Be cautious of all medication and drugs that can cause liver damage.

- Avoid, or severely restrict, alcohol intake.

- Remind doctors, dentists, and healthcare providers that they are carriers.

- Cover all cuts and open sores with a bandage.

- Wipe up blood spills, and then clean the area with an approved disinfectant.

- Not donate blood, plasma, body organs, tissue, or sperm if you are infected.

- Not share toothbrushes, razors, needles, syringes, nail files, clippers, scissors, or any object, which may come into contact with your blood or body fluids.

- Throw away personal items, such as tissues, menstrual pads, tampons, or bandages in a plastic bag.

A CAUTION AGAINST THE USE OF ALCOHOL

Alcohol plays a major role in the progression of chronic hepatitis. Not only is it capable of damaging the liver on its own, there is evidence that it might lead to an increase in the amount of circulating virus. Therefore, all hepatitis carriers should be strongly cautioned against drinking alcohol, or other activities that affect the liver, such as taking drugs.

OBJECTIVES

At this time, you should be able to:

- Identify the viral strains of hepatitis discussed in the lesson.

- Name the functions of the liver discussed in the lesson.

- Discuss the different transmission routes for each of the viral strains of Hepatitis

Pathway to an *Addiction Free* Lifestyle

THE ABC'S OF HEPATITIS

	Hepatitis A (HAV)	**Hepatitis B (HBV)**	**Hepatitis C (HCV)**	**Hepatitis D (HDV)**	**Hepatitis E (HEV)**
What is it?	HAV is a virus that causes inflammation of the liver. It does not lead to chronic disease	HIV is a virus that causes inflammation of the liver. It can cause liver cell damage, leading to cirrhosis and cancer.	HCV is a virus that causes inflammation of the liver. It can cause liver cell damage, leading to cirrhosis and cancer.	HDV is a virus that causes inflammation of the liver. It only infects those persons with HBV.	HEV is a virus that causes inflammation of the liver. It is rare in the US. There is no chronic state.
Incubation period	2 to 7 weeks. Average 4 weeks.	6 to 23 weeks. Average 17 weeks.	2 to 25 weeks. Average 7 to 9 weeks.	2 to 8 weeks.	2 to 9 weeks. Average 40 days.
How is it spread?	Transmitted by fecal/oral route, through close person-to-person contact or ingestion of contaminated food and water.	Contact with infected blood, seminal fluid, vaginal secretions, contaminated needles, including tattoo and body-piercing tools. Infected mother to newborn. Human bite. Sexual contact.	Contact with infected blood, contaminated IV needles, razors, and tattoo or body-piercing tools. Infected mother to newborn. Human Bite. Not easily spread through sex.	Contact with infected blood, contaminated needles. Sexual contact with HDV infected person.	Transmitted through fecal/oral route. Outbreaks associated with contaminated water supply in other countries.
Symptoms	May have none. Others may have light stools, dark urine, fatigue, fever, nausea, vomiting, abdominal pain, and jaundice.	May have none. Some persons have mild-flu-like symptoms, dark urine, light stools, jaundice, fatigue and fever.	Same as HBV.	Same as HBV.	Same as HBV.
Treatment of Chronic Disease	Not applicable.	Interferon and Lamivudine with varying success.	Interferon and combination therapies with varying success.	Interferon with varying success.	Not applicable.
Vaccine	Two doses of vaccine to anyone over 2 years of age.	Three doses may be given to person of any age.	None	HBV vaccine prevents HDV infection.	None.
Who is at risk?	Household or sexual contact with an infected person or living in an area with HAV outbreak. Travelers to developing countries, person engaging in anal/oral sex and injection drug users.	Infants born to infected mother, having sex with an infected person or multiple partners, injection drug users, emergency responders, healthcare workers, persons engaging in anal/oral sex and hemodialysis patients.	Anyone who had a blood transfusion before 1990, healthcare workers, IV drug users, hemodialysis patients, infants born to infected mother, and multiple sex partners.	Injection drug users, persons engaging in anal/oral sex with those having sex with an HDV infected person.	Travelers to developing countries, especially pregnant women.
Prevention	Immune Globulin within 2 weeks of exposure. Vaccination. Washing hands with soap and water after going to the toilet. Use of household bleach (10 parts water to 1 part bleach) to clean surfaces contaminated with feces, such as changing tables. Safe sex.	Immune Globulin within 2 weeks of exposure. Vaccination provides protection for 18 years. Clean up infected blood with household bleach and wear protective gloves. Do not share razors, toothbrushes or needles. Safe sex.	Clean up spilled blood with household bleach. Wear gloves when touching blood. Do not share razors, toothbrushes, or needles with anyone. Safe sex.	Hepatitis B vaccine to prevent HBV infection. Safe sex.	Avoid drinking or using potentially contaminated water.

Pathway to an *Addiction Free* Lifestyle

Pathway to an *Addiction Free* Lifestyle
LIVING WITH HEPATITIS C

SELF-HELP TIPS

Frequently, people learn that they have HCV from a blood test during a routine physical or because they have donated blood. While testing, positive is not good news; however, it is not all doom and gloom or a death sentence. Here are some important things to remember.

Don't Panic. In most people the infection does not disappear, so you need to learn to live with it. Think positively. Many people live 20 - 40 years with the virus without becoming seriously ill or having liver failure.

Get regular medical attention. A physician who knows about HCV, a gastroenterologist or hepatologist, can watch for signs of trouble, identify problems and keep you informed about new treatments.

Avoid contact with blood. HCV can be transmitted by blood. Cover open cuts and don't share razors, toothbrushes, manicure tools, needles, or anything that might have even the smallest amount of blood on it. Be wary of menstrual blood as well.

Protect your liver. Your liver is already stressed by the hepatitis virus. Omit or severely limit alcohol use. Alcohol should not be taken with other drugs and especially acetaminophen, the ingredient in Tylenol, and a number of other headache and cold remedies. The combination may damage your liver that is already trying to fight off the virus. Check with your doctor before using any medications, including over-the-counter drugs or alternative medicines.

Be concerned about sex partners. While studies have shown the risk of sexual transmission is low between long-term, monogamous couples, people with new or multiple sexual partners should use latex condoms. Inform potential partners that you have the virus. In addition, viral levels in the blood can vary widely or rise in response to immunosuppressive drugs, which would make HCV carriers more infectious at certain times. Virus levels increase when certain medications such as corticosteroids or cyclosporine are taken. People with HCV who take these drugs should discuss precautions needed with their doctor.

Be informed. Keep yourself updated on current research, information, and treatment. Be aware of your own health status and what your various options are.

Pathway to an *Addiction Free* Lifestyle
Hepatitis Test

1. Which are viral strains of Hepatitis?

    A. A, F, X, Y, Z

    B. A, B, C, D, E

    C. C, D, O, P, S

    D. A, E, I, O, U

2. It is easier to be exposed to Hepatitis.

    A. A & C

    B. C & D

    C. A & E

3. The functions of the liver include

    A. Converting food into energy

    B. Assisting in making clotting factors

    C. Produce Bile

    D. Removing poisonous waste from blood

    E. All of the above

4. Which of the following forms of Hepatitis are transmitted by the fecal-oral route and through food handlers?

    A. Hepatitis A

    B. Hepatitis B

    C. Hepatitis C

    D. Hepatitis D

5. Hepatitis C can live in blood found on razors, clippers, and needles.

    A. True

    B. False

6. Hepatitis is an inflammation of the

    A. Pancreas

    B. Kidney

    C. Liver

    D. Lymphatic System

7. Hepatitis C is a blood borne pathogen.

    A. True

    B. False

8. Which of the following symptoms is not normally consistent with Hepatitis infection

    A. Fatigue

    B. Nausea and vomiting

    C. Yellowing of the eyes and skin

    D. Kaposi's Sarcoma

9. People with Hepatitis infection:

    A. Cannot spread Hepatitis to others

    B. Have no symptoms

    C. Have a virus

    D. All of the above

10. Which type of hepatitis is commonly transmitted through food handlers?

    A. Hepatitis A

    B. Hepatitis B

    C. Hepatitis C

    D. Hepatitis D

Answers:

(1) B (2) C (3) E (4) A (5) A (6) C (7) A (8) D (9) C (10) A

Pathway to an *Addiction Free* Lifestyle

Pathway to an *Addiction Free* Lifestyle

PEER EDUCATION PROGRAM

HIV/AIDS

This information is not meant to replace the medical counsel of your doctor or individual consultation with a registered dietitian. This information is informational and may only be used in its entirety.

Pathway to an *Addiction Free* Lifestyle

OVERVIEW

HIV / AIDS

As recently as a few decades ago it was widely believed that infectious diseases were not as much of a public health threat as conditions like cancer and heart disease. Breakthroughs had been made in modern medicine that eradicated smallpox and conquered syphilis.

The sudden appearance and rapid spread of a previously unknown deadly infectious disease given the name of Acquired Immune Deficiency Syndrome (AIDS) soon raised a series of compelling questions: What is AIDS? What is the cause? Where did it come from? Who is at risk for getting infected?

Today we live in the shadows of AIDS. More than 30 years after the first rumors of "gay plague" spread through the bathhouses of New York and San Francisco, over 64.3 million people worldwide — gay and straight alike — have been infected by the Human Immunodeficiency Virus (HIV). This virus causes, what has been, until recently a fatal disease in which nearly 25 million people worldwide have died

We are here to acquire a deeper understanding of the nature and course of HIV and AIDS.

OBJECTIVES

By the end of this class, you will be able to:

- Describe the difference between HIV and AIDS.
- Discuss the origin of HIV/AIDS.
- Identify the transmission routes for HIV infection and identify who is at risk.
- Compare the three results of HIV antibody tests.
- Identify five symptoms of HIV.
- Identify three methods of prevention against HIV.
- Identify treatment methods.

OBJECTIVES
- ✓ Describe the difference between HIV and AIDS.
- ✓ Discuss the origin of HIV/AIDS.
- ✓ Identify the transmission routes for HIV infection and identify who is at risk.
- ✓ Compare the three results of HIV antibody tests.
- ✓ Identify five symptoms of HIV.
- ✓ Identify three methods of prevention against HIV.
- ✓ Identify treatment methods.

WHAT IS AIDS? WHAT IS HIV?

Acquired Immune Deficiency Syndrome (AIDS)
- ✓ Body's ability to fight infection impaired
- ✓ Acquired from exposure to infected person
- ✓ Natural defense system not working
- ✓ Number of symptoms occurring together

AIDS is an acronym for **Acquired Immune Deficiency Syndrome**. This means the body's ability to fight disease has been impaired, leaving the affected individual vulnerable to illnesses that a healthy immune system can overcome. The name appropriately defines the condition. It is "acquired" from exposure to an infected person. "Immune deficiency" refers to the body's natural system of defense is not functioning normally. "Syndrome' means occurs together characterizing a specific disease or disorder.

HIV is the name of the virus that can lead to full-blown AIDS. It stands for **Human Immunodeficiency Virus**. The HIV virus is an aggressive virus that invades the human body, and quickly reproduces itself inside the body's immune cells until they are destroyed. Although the immune system will usually mount a strong defense, it is no match for HIV. As HIV depletes more and more infection-fighting cells in the body, and more viruses are produced, the body weakens and becomes vulnerable to opportunistic infections. This means the body is now susceptible to a number of unusual diseases that rarely infect those with normal immunity. For example, microorganisms found in ordinary tap water or in the soil can threaten the health and life of an HIV-infected person if the CD4 count is below normal.

What is HIV	
H	Human
I	Immunodeficiency
V	Virus

Human Immunodeficiency Virus (HIV)
- ✓ Aggressive virus
- ✓ Invades immune cells
- ✓ Reproduces
- ✓ Weakens immune system
- ✓ Leads to AIDS

When these opportunistic infections occur, the person is said to have AIDS or is CD4 count below 200 even without infections. In other words, people die from all the diseases they can acquire due to an impaired immune system, not from the virus.

THE ORIGIN OF AIDS

Medical researchers are still baffled by the origin of the AIDS epidemic. One theory is that AIDS started through contact with infected monkeys in remote areas of Africa and spread to the rest of the population through urbanization and mass immunization projects.

> **ORIGIN OF AIDS**
> ✓ Isolated 1983
> ✓ First retrovirus to infect humans
> ✓ Exact origin unknown

A recent discovery of the oldest known HIV blood sample found in Zaire that was frozen from a study that occurred in 1959 suggests the virus jumped from animals to humans in the 1940's.

Scientists had never seen a virus exactly like HIV prior to the discovery in 1983. HIV is one of the first retroviruses (virus that carry their genetic information in RNA rather than DNA, and the RNA information must be translated "Backwards" into DNA) to infect humans and is closely related to a monkey retrovirus, Simian Immunodeficiency Virus (SIV)." Monkeys and apes are often the only animal species other than human beings that are infected with human viruses such as yellow fever, Marburg and the Ebola virus. What is not understood is why this retrovirus is benign (not recurrent or progressive) in some animals but lethal in human beings.

For example, the African Green Monkey is a major reservoir of the SIV. While SIV does not cause disease in the infected green monkeys, it does cause Simian AIDS if certain monkeys are inoculated with the virus. Medical researchers continue to speculate as critical debate lingers on the HIV/AIDS hypothesis. Meanwhile, this will not be the first time in human history for a mysterious epidemic to come along, devastate a population and disappear.

HIV/AIDS Timeline

In the United States, the early mystery of the epidemiology of the HIV epidemic began to unravel as more people became infected.

On **June 5, 1981**, U.S. physicians read for the first time of a curious new health problem in homosexual Americans in the Morbidity and Mortality Weekly Report published by the Centers for Disease Control and Prevention (CDC).

A Los Angeles physician, Dr. Michael Gottlieb, reported the occurrence of pneumocystis pneumonia in five previously healthy individuals. For Gottlieb, his diagnosis was at first inconceivable. These patients also suffered from other strange illnesses (i.e. Cytomegalovirus (CMV), Candida albicans) rarely found in healthy young men. Moreover, results from their blood tests only deepened the mystery; the patient's T-cell response was almost none.

July 1982 — Faced with a growing number of cases among homosexuals, intravenous drug users and hemophiliacs, in which the immune system collapses for no apparent reason, U.S. health officials coined the term AIDS (Acquired Immune Deficiency Syndrome) for the new disease.

December 1982 — The first documented case of AIDS resulting from a blood transfusion leads to a government warning that the blood supply might be contaminated.

May 1983 - Luc Montagnier and a team of researchers of the Pasteur Institute of Paris reported that a human retrovirus might cause AIDS.

April 1984 - Dr. Robert Gallo, of the National Cancer Institute in Bethesda, Maryland, announced that his laboratory has also isolated the AIDS virus.

March 1985 - U.S. Food and Drug Administration approved the first AIDS antibody test. which is immediately used to screen the nation's blood supply.

March 1987 - The FDA approves AZT as the first antiretroviral drug to fight AIDS.

April 1990 - The death of Ryan White, 18, a hemophiliac who had contracted AIDS from tainted blood, and who was ostracized in his Indiana hometown, became a symbol of AIDS intolerance.

June 1991 - A decade into the epidemic, the Centers for Disease Control and Prevention (CDC) reports that one million Americans are infected with HIV. At this point, half of the 500,000 people in the Western Hemisphere with AIDS have died.

HIV STRAINS AND REINFECTION

HIV Strains
Two different virus
- ✓ HIV-1, Epidemic in US
- ✓ HIV-2, Epidemic in Africa

There are two main strains of the HIV virus, HIV-1 and HIV-2. When no strain is given, it is commonly referring to HIV-1. HIV-1 is more common in the Western Hemisphere, Europe, Asia, and most of Africa. HIV-2 is more prevalent in West Africa; it is transmitted less easily and progresses less quickly to AIDS than HIV-1. Some people are co-infected with both HIV viruses.

HIV-1 is responsible for most AIDS cases. The HIV epidemic in the United States and other western countries is caused by this viral strain.

HIV-1 is divided into three groups, group M, group N, and group 0. Group M is further subdivided into at least five subtypes, subtype A, found in Africa; subtype B, found in Europe and the United States; subtype C & D, both of which are found in Africa; subtype E, which is found in Southeast Asia, especially Thailand; and, subtype G, a recombinant form found in Kenya. About 95% of all HIV falls into in of these HIV-1 subtypes.

Re-infection can occur if an HIV-positive person acquires another subtype or a more virulent (infectious) strain of HIV from another HIV-infected person.

HIV SYMPTOMS

- Prolonged, unexplained fatigue
- Swollen glands (lymph nodes)
- Chills
- Excessive sweating especially night sweats
- Mouth lesion including yeast lesions and painful swollen gums
- Sore throat
- Cough
- Shortness of breath
- Changes in bowel habits including constipation
- Frequent diarrhea
- Symptoms of a specific opportunistic infection
- Tumor (Kaposi sarcoma) [skin cancer]
- Skin rashes or lesions of various types
- Unintentional weight loss
- General discomfort or uneasiness (malaise)
- Headache

TRANSMISSION

Routes of exposure to HIV occur through the bodily fluids of an HIV-infected person. Let's discuss the body fluids, the sites where the virus can be transmitted, and the behaviors that can lead to infection.

> **Transmission**
> Where does the virus live inside the body?
> ✓ Blood
> ✓ Body fluids containing blood
> ✓ Semen, vaginal secretions
> ✓ Breast milk

> **Transmission**
> Fluids that transmit HIV
> ✓ Blood
> ✓ Any bodily fluid containing visible blood
> ✓ Semen
> ✓ Vaginal Secretions
> ✓ Cerebrospinal fluid (Brain & spinal cord)
> ✓ Synovial fluid (surrounding joints)
> ✓ Peritoneal fluid in membranes lining the abdominal/pelvic walls
> ✓ Pericardial fluid surrounding the heart
> ✓ Amniotic fluid (serous fluid in which the fetus/baby is suspended
> ✓ Human breast milk (mother to baby)

Body fluids

HIV has been isolated in many different body fluids, and Prevention (CDC) recommends precautions be taken with the following fluids:

- Blood
- Any bodily fluid containing visible blood
- Semen
- Vaginal secretions
- Cerebrospinal fluid (brain and spinal cord)
- Synovial fluid (surrounding joints)
- Pleural fluid (surrounding membranes of lungs and thoracic cavity)
- Peritoneal fluid (in membranes lining abdominal/pelvic walls)
- Pericardial fluid (surrounding the heart)
- Amniotic fluid (serous fluid in which the fetus/baby is suspended)
- Human breast milk (mother to baby)

Menstrual blood would be included in "blood" on this list. It is considered to have a high concentration of virus.

Although HIV has been detected in the following fluids, the viral concentrations **are not** sufficient to cause transmission (unless visible blood is present): tears, saliva, urine, feces, vomit, sputum, nasal secretions, and sweat.

Pathway to an *Addiction Free* Lifestyle

Infected Sites

> **INFECTION SITES**
> - Mucous membranes, mouth, nose, eyes, genitals
> - Broken skin, cuts or opened, abraded skin
> - Punctures, needle sticks/sharing, bites

Mucous membranes: mouth, nose, eyes, genitals

Broken skin: cuts; or opened, abraded skin (abrasions)

Punctures: needle sticks, bites, needle sharing

Risky Behaviors

- Needle Sharing: sharing the syringe, or blood-soaked cotton of an infected person.

- Sex: having sex with and HIV-infected person. The sex can be oral, vaginal, or anal.

- Tattoos: needles and ink used during the tattoo process are capable of transmitting the virus.

- Blood Rituals: commingling blood with an infected person can transmit HIV.

- Body Piercing: piercing equipment used on an infected person is capable of transmitting HIV.

High Risk Activities

- Perinatal: an HIV-infected mother can transmit the virus to her fetus

- Blood Transfusion: it is possible to receive blood, which has been poorly screened

- Health Care Workers: handling waste materials, needles or attending to an HIV-infected person's personal protective equipment can lead to infection

> **Behaviors**
> - Needle sharing
> - Sex with an infected person
> - Tattoos
> - Blood rituals
> - Body piercing
> - Blood transfusion

Pathway to an *Addiction Free* Lifestyle
PREVENTION: HIV RISK ELIMINATION AND HARM REDUCTION

Now that we understand the exchange of body fluids that transmit the virus, it should be more readily apparent that the risk of becoming HIV infected could indeed be eliminated or reduced.

Let us first discuss the many ways we can eliminate the risk:

PREVENTION
- ✓ Sexual abstinence
- ✓ Monogamous sex
- ✓ Latex condom with water based lubricant for anal and vaginal sex
- ✓ Dental dam for oral sex
- ✓ Do not acquire tattoo or body piercing
- ✓ Observe universal precaution

Risk Elimination

- Practice sexual abstinence

- Engage in monogamous sex between two partners (having only one sexual partner)

- Kiss, hug, and arouse with mutual masturbation (avoid kissing, especially, If partner has open sores in the mouth)

- Use a latex condom with a water-based lubricant such as K-Y jelly for anal or vaginal sex. Oil-based lubricants like Vaseline have been known to weaken condoms

- During sex, men should pull out and avoid ejaculating inside their partner, even when using a condom. If you do ejaculate, hold the condom during withdrawal to keep semen from spilling

- If a condom breaks during sex, immediately replace it with a new one

- Use dental dams for vaginal oral sex

- Use a fresh condom with sex toys

- Do not acquire tattoos or body piercing. Temporary tattoos are available that are applied with water or vegetable dyes

Observe universal precautions when exposed to blood or when caring for an HIV-infected person

To practice **universal precautions**, we must always assume that all body fluids, open wounds, lesions, etc. of all persons are infectious. Therefore, appropriate steps should be taken to place a barrier between these fluids and portals of entry on our bodies. Wearing latex gloves, covering cuts with bandages and learning how to reduce exposure on the job, can achieve this.

Still, we have to recognize that this is not a perfect world. Sexual encounters and being under the influence of drugs and alcohol can have people doing things they normally would not do under other circumstances. In situations like these, it is important to consider how the risk of transmission can be reduced.

Harm Reduction
- ✓ Avoid dirty needles
- ✓ Use bleaching agents to clean tattoo guns and body piercing equipment
- ✓ Don't use alcohol or drugs; it impairs judgment
- ✓ Get frequent checkups
- ✓ Support groups

Harm Reduction

- Avoid dirty needles and needle stick injuries

- Use bleaching agents, not alcohol, to clean tattoo guns and body piercing equipment

- Learn to minimize the heavy use of alcohol or drugs that impair your judgment in sexual situations

- Get frequent checkups if sexually active (will not reduce your risk)

- Consider support groups or counseling to help you stay safe

HIV EFFECTS ON THE IMMUNE SYSTEM

Higher levels of virus referred to as **viral load**; appear to be associated with a lower number of T-cells. In contrast, lower viral counts usually mean higher T-cell counts. In as little as 10 days after infection, HIV-infected persons can experience flu-like symptoms (fever, fatigue, ect.) as the virus circulates. T-cell counts can remain high for a long time as the immune system works to remove the virus from the blood. For years, virus levels are reduced, but replication is constant. HIV levels will continue to increase as the disease progresses. Eventually opportunistic infections occur as T-cell counts dramatically drop.

A 'normal' T-cell count would be in the 600-1400 range. Persons with HIV disease who have T-cell counts below 200 are given an AIDS diagnosis even without opportunistic infections.

OPPORTUNISTIC INFECTIONS

An individual is diagnosed with AIDS when he/she has had at least two opportunistic infections (01) or CD4<200. The main 01's are Tuberculosis (TB), Pneumocystis Carinii Pneumonia (PCP), Cancer (Kaposi's sarcoma), toxoplasmosis, Mycobacterium Avium Complex (MAC), Cytomegalovirus (CMV), and Candidiasis.

HIV SCREENING AND TESTING

AIDS is a frightening disease, but today there are new therapies and approaches that are keeping many people with HIV healthy. The key is early intervention/early **detection** of those perceived to be at risk. Early intervention refers to the screening for HIV and the use of treatments to slow the progression of the virus early on in the infection.

In the community, HIV tests are done free of charge by the health department as well as many healthcare agencies. In the institutions, tests are free but voluntary, so they have to be requested.

> **SCREENING AND TESTING**
> ✓ Early intervention of those at risk
> ✓ Blood screening by ELISA, which identifies the presence of HIV antibodies
> ✓ This test is 99% effective
> ✓ Blood confirmation test is the Western Blot
> ✓ If unable to confirm repeat

HIV tests are done using an enzyme-linked immunoassay ("**ELISA**" test) performed on blood. The test seeks to identify the presence of **HIV antibodies** (proteins produced by plasma cells in response to a specific foreign organism). The ELISA test is considered 99% reliable. These results, however, are confirmed with a "**Western Blot**" screening test. In the rare event that the Western Blot cannot confirm the ELISA results, it is recommended that the testing process begin again.

Antibody — Positive Test Result

> **TESTING**
> ✓ Positive Test
> ✓ Antibodies to HIV have been founded in the blood
> ✓ Does not mean subject has AIDS

A positive test result means antibodies to HIV have been found in the blood. This means the test subject has been exposed to and is infected with the virus and the body has produced antibodies. It does not mean that the person has AIDS or will necessarily develop AIDS in the near future.

People with a positive test result are infectious and capable of passing the virus to others through sexual contact and sharing needles and syringes. Safer or protected sex is a must, not only because the person could expose someone else, but also re-exposure to the virus may increase chances of developing AIDS.

Antibody — Negative Test Result

A negative test result means that no antibodies have been found in the blood at the present time. The reasons for this may be:

- The person has not been exposed to the virus

- The person has been exposed, but antibodies have not yet been produced: or

- The test may be a false negative, which rarely occurs

> **Testing**
> Negative test
> No antibodies found in blood
> Why:
> - Has not been exposed
> - False negative
> - Exposed by too early for production of antibodies

High-risk individuals should consider follow-up retesting.

Indeterminate Test Results

On occasion, a person will receive an indeterminate test result. There are various reasons for an indeterminate:

> **Testing**
> Indeterminate test
> ✓ Antibodies not high enough to indicate positive test
> ✓ Test kit may be too sensitive
> ✓ Follow-up test recommended

- The level of antibodies was not high enough to indicate a positive result because antibodies are just beginning to form

- Perhaps the test kit was too sensitive

In the case of indeterminate test results, a follow-up test is recommended. Often antibodies do not appear on the ELISA test during the first 6-12 weeks following infection; sometimes the period extends to six months or more. Because of this phenomenon, the first six months are referred to as the 'window period'. Meanwhile the person is infected and can infect others.

At six months, 95% of all tests will reveal antibodies if they are present. In the rare case, it may take an additional 6-12 months to reveal the antibodies.

In the State of California, HIV Post-Test Counseling is given to all persons who test positive for HIV. This is a mandatory counseling session because of the tremendous emotional response that may occur when one learns of their positive test results.

In the California Department of Corrections and Rehabilitation, with few exceptions, HIV screens are voluntary. In 1995, over 27.000 voluntary tests were performed.

In 1996, the Federal Drug Administration approved an oral HIV ELISA screening test, which measures the presence of HIV antibodies in cell tissue from the gum line. This new test will reduce the risk of needle stick injury for health care personnel along with the need to draw blood for the ELISA test.

TREATMENT OF HIV

Treatment of patients infected with HIV changed enormously in 1996. Previously it was believed the virus remained latent for many years. HIV is now known to produce high rates of viral replication and death of immune cells soon after infection. "Hit early, hit hard" is the new strategy for the treatment of HIV.

Treatment
✓ Hit early; hit hard
✓ Combination therapy

Use of potent combination therapy known as HAART (highly active antiretroviral therapy) has been associated with dramatic decreases in incidences of AIDS.

Combination therapy, commonly called "cocktails," to fight against HIV typically includes a regimen of **Reverse Transcriptase** (AZT-like drugs) drugs to attack the virus before it has the opportunity to infect a cell and reprogram it to produce more viruses. The **Protease Inhibitors** block the part of HIV that is called "protease." This is done so that when the virus begins to create more copies of itself, the copies are defective in a sense in that they are not capable of infecting new cells. In addition, protease inhibitors have been shown to be less toxic and have fewer side effects.

TREATMENT
HIV
CD4 count above 200
AIDS
CD4 count below 200

Studies have shown that protease inhibitors can reduce the amount of virus in the blood and increase T4 cell counts. In some cases, these drugs improved T4 cell counts even when they were very low. However, these effects can wear off over time. This happens because HIV makes more of itself all the time, and each new virus that is made is slightly different. This is likely to develop into what medical scientists call resistance.

CHALLENGES OF THE HIV EPIDEMIC

TREATMENT
✓ Medical history it Complete physical
✓ Complete blood screening
✓ A May include skin test for TB
✓ Drug therapy

Through unprecedented global attention and intervention efforts, the rate of new HIV infections has slowed and prevalence rates have leveled off globally and in many regions. Despite the progress seen in some countries and regions, the total number of people living with HIV continues to rise. What lies ahead are challenges that will take us far into this century.

- The cost of cocktails puts them beyond the reach of all but the best-insured patients; and out of the question for the 90% of HIV-infected individuals who live in developing nations.

- Though the number of children on antiretrovirals (ARVs) has risen, many more lack treatment. Obstacles include access to appropriate and affordable pediatric drugs that are easy to store and prepare in resource-scarce settings.

- Difficulties for a vaccine to stop the global pandemic include the fact that HIV mutates so quickly; the virus targets the immune response, which is normally stimulated to create immunity; and vaccines need to be administered prior to infection in order to gain protection from them.

Pathway to an Addiction Free Lifestyle

- HIV/AIDS disproportionately infects populations that lack the power or means to protect themselves. Women, children and young people are at-risk because of their age and gender; commercial sex workers, injection drug users, men who have sex with men and prisoners may have limited access to condoms or clean needles.

- Global funding is increasing, but global need is growing even faster — widening the funding gap. Services and funding are disproportionate.

- Too many persons continue to be diagnosed with HIV late in the course of their infection and miss opportunities for treatment and prevention. In 2008, 1/3 (32%) of individuals with an HIV diagnosis reported to the CDC received a diagnosis of AIDS within 12 months of their initial HIV diagnosis.

- Globally the impact of HIV/AIDS on women and girls has been particularly devastating. Women and girls now comprise 50% of those aged 15 and older living with HIV.

- HIV infections and AIDS deaths are unevenly distributed geographically and the nature of the epidemics vary by region. Epidemics are abating in some countries and burgeoning in others. More than 90% of people with HIV are living in the developing world.

- Also, now that there is hope, there is risk for individuals who perceive there is "a cure'. for AIDS who are returning to high-risk behaviors. Therefore, our only hope to stop the spread of HIV and AIDS is to break the chain of infection by practicing safe sex, not sharing needles, adopting a healthy lifestyle, as well as raising the level of awareness in future generations to come.

REVIEW MAJOR POINTS
- HIV can elect ANYONE
- HIV is not transmitted through casual contact or kissing
- Y. No one has ever gotten HIV through biting
- Mosquitoes and other insect's can not transmit HIV
- Dentists and physicians do not transmit HIV to patient's Rich peep* don't have the CUM WI AIDS. No one has the cure for AIDS

OBJECTIVES
- Describe the difference between HIV and AIDS
- Discuss the origin of HIV/AIDS
- Identify the transmission routes for HIV infection and identify who is at risk
- Compare the three results of HIV antibody tests
- Identify five symptoms of HIV
- Identify three methods of prevention against HIV
- Identify treatment methods

Time Magazine, February 16, 1998. 'When Did AIDS Begin?"
Retroviruses, like HIV, reproduce by copying their genetic material, RNA, directly into the DNA of a cell.

Pathway to an *Addiction Free* Lifestyle

STATISTICS

California:

- Nearly 200,000 Californians have contracted HIV/AIDS and nearly 90,000 have died since the epidemic began in the early 1980s.

- California ranks second in the nation in cumulative AIDS cases at 157,719, surpassed only by New York.

- Approximately 109,000 Californians are HIV-positive, among whom 69,728 are living with AIDS.

- There are 7,000 new HIV infections in the state every year.

- In California, 75.7% of all HIV/AIDS cases occur among gay men, far exceeding the 53% nationally.

- Men make up 89.5%. Women account for 9.8% of cases, and transgender persons for 0.6%.

- Of all HIV cases, Whites account for 46.7% followed by Hispanics at 29.2% and African Americans at 18.9%.

- More than 60% of Californians living with HIV reside in Los Angeles County or the San Francisco Bay Area. Source: California Office of AIDS, AIDS Surveillance Report (as of June 2010).

United States:

- CDC estimates that 1.1 million people are living with HIV in the U.S. One in five (21%) of those people are unaware of their infection.

- Every 9 1/2 minutes, someone in the U.S. is infected with HIV.

- An estimated 56,300 Americans become infected with HIV each year.

- According to the CDC 11,295 deaths occurred from HIV-infection in 2007.

- Through 2007, 583,298 people with AIDS in the U.S. have died of AIDS-related causes.

- Each year, approximately 16-22 million persons in the United States are tested for HIV.

- In 2002, an estimated 38-44% of all adults had been tested for HIV.

- Injection drug use has directly and indirectly accounted for more than 36% of AIDS cases in the United States since the epidemic began.

- During 1997, 20-26% of all people living with HIV in the U.S. passed through a correctional facility.

United States statistics by Risk Group:

- Individuals infected through heterosexual contact account for 31% of annual new HIV infections and 28% of people living with HIV.

- Women account for 27% of annual new HIV infections and 25% of those living with HIV.

- Injection drug users represent 12% of annual new HIV infections and 19% of those living with HIV:

- Men Who Have Sex with Men (MSM) account for more than half (53%) of all new HIV infections, as well as nearly half (48%) of people living with HIV.

- The rate of new HIV diagnoses among MSM is more than 44 times that of other men and more than 40 times that of women.

- White MSM account for the largest number of annual new HIV infections of any group in the U.S., followed closely by black MSM.

- The largest number of new infections among white MSM occurred in those aged 3039 years, followed by those aged 40-49 years.

- Among all African American/Black MSM, there were more new HIV infections (52%) among young African American/Black MSM (aged 13-29 years) than any other racial or ethnic age group of MSM in 2006.

- MSM is the only risk group in the U.S. in which new HIV infections have been increasing since the early 1990's.

- In 2006, more than 30,000 MSM and MSM IDU were newly infected with HIV.

- In 2007, MSM were 44 to 86 times as likely to be diagnosed with HIV compared with other men, and 40 to 77 times as likely as women.

United States statistics by Race/Ethnicity:

- African Americans/Blacks face the most severe burden of HIV and AIDS in the nation.

Pathway to an *Addiction Free* Lifestyle

- African Americans/Blacks account for almost half (46%) of people living with HIV in the U.S., as well as nearly half (45%) of new infections each year.

- Approximately one in 16 African American/Black men will be diagnosed with HIV, as will one in 30 African American/Black women.

- The rate of new HIV infections for African American/Black men is about six times as high as that of white men, nearly three times that of Hispanic/Latino men, and more than twice that of African American/Black women.

- The HIV incidence rate for African American/Black women is nearly 15 times as high as that of white women, and nearly four times that of Hispanic/Latina women.

- HIV/AIDS is a leading cause of death among African Americans/Blacks ages 24-44.

- Hispanics/Latinos account for and estimated 17% of people living with HIV and 17% of new infections.

- One in 36 Hispanic/Latino men will be diagnosed with HIV, as will 1 in 106 Hispanic/Latina women.

- The rate of new HIV infections among Hispanic/Latino men is more than double that of white men and the rate among Hispanic/Latina women is nearly four times that of white women.

- The rate of HIV infections among Hispanic/Latinos in 2006 was 2.5 times that of whites.

- In 2004, one in five people living with AIDS in the U.S. was Latino.

- In 2005, 65% of people diagnosed with HIV/AIDS were African American/Black or Latino.

- New HIV infections in the United States:

- In 2006, Hispanic/Latino men made up three quarters (76%) of new infections among all Hispanic/Latinos. The rate of new infections among Hispanic/Latino men was more than double that of white men.

- In 2006, Hispanic/Latino men who have sex with men (MSM) represented 72% of new infections among all Hispanic/Latino men, and nearly 19% among all MSM. Among Hispanic/Latino MSM, 43% occurred in Hispanic/Latino MSM under age 30, and the remaining 57% occurred in Hispanic/Latino

- While Hispanic/Latino women represented a quarter (24%) of new infections among Hispanics/Latinos in 2006, their rate of HIV infection was nearly four times that of white women.

- The number of new infections among young black MSM was nearly twice that of young white MSM and more than twice that of young Hispanic/Latino MSM.

- Among all Hispanic/Latino MSM in 2006, the largest number of new infections (43%) occurred in the youngest age group (13-29 years), though a substantial number of new HIV infections (35%) were among those aged 30-35 years.

HIV and AIDS Diagnoses and Deaths in the United States:

- In 2008, Hispanics/Latinos accounted for more than 19% of the 42,439 new diagnoses of HIV infection in the 37 states and 5 U.S. dependent areas with confidential name-based HIV infection reporting.

- In 2008, an estimated 7,864 Hispanics/Latinos were diagnosed with AIDS in the U.S. and dependent areas.

- By the end of 2007, and estimated 106,074 Hispanics/Latinos with AIDS diagnosis had died in the US and dependent areas.

- In 2007, HIV was the fifth leading cause of death among Hispanics/Latinos aged 3544 and the sixth leading cause of death among Hispanics/Latinos aged 25-34 in the U.S.

- Hispanics/Latinos are most likely to be infected with HIV as a result of sexual contact with men.

- In five different studies Hispanics/Latinos were reported to have the highest rates of unprotected male-to-male sexual contact.

HIV/AIDS and STDs

- Syphilis, genital herpes type 2, chancroid, and other infections that cause genital or rectal ulcers may increase the risk of HIV transmission per sexual exposure 10 to 50 times for male-to-female transmission and 50 to 300 times for female-to-male exposure.

- Nonulcerative STDs (e.g., chlamydia and gonorrhea) have been shown to increase the risk of HIV transmission by two-fold to five-fold.

- Treatment of gonorrhea in HIV-infected men reduces the prevalence of HIV shedding in urethral secretions by approximately 50%.

HIV/AIDS and TB

- The risk of acquiring tuberculosis is 20 to 37 times greater among HIV positive individuals.

- TB is a leading cause of death among people who are HIV-positive.

- About 1/3 of the of the 33.2 million HIV-positive people worldwide are co-infected with TB and one in four people living with HIV die as a result of TB.

HIV/AIDS and HEPATITIS C

- About one quarter of HIV-infected persons in the United States are also infected with hepatitis C virus (HCV).

- Co-infection with HIV and HCV is common among HIV-infected injection drug users (IUDs), between 50-90%.

Pathway to an *Addiction Free* Lifestyle

"WHAT IF..."
An activity on HIV/AIDS

This part of the training can be invaluable in terms of "clearing up" lingering doubts that the peer educators may have about HIV disease and AIDS. It is a chance for an open dialogue that will help you straighten out those HIV/AIDS myths that have been around the prison for years.

What if?

...I'm injured during a fight?

Remember to keep any blood away from the eyes, mouth, cuts, and open sores. After a fight, try to wash off any other person's blood you might have on your body. If you come in contact with another person's blood, seek medical help.

...I know one or more of my cellies have HIV/AIDS?

You're in no danger. Just avoid contact with blood and semen. Anything else is not infectious.

...And that person doesn't want to tell?

That is their business. However, suggest the inmate see a doctor, or get him to talk to a peer educator.

...I don't have extra personal items, like toothbrushes and razors and I have to use someone else's?

Don't use anyone's razor or toothbrush. Toothbrushes and razors can be distributed to inmates. Ask for replacements. Just ask any Correctional Officer about it.

...I'm seriously drug addicted?

The CDCR cannot give drugs to inmates. If you have a drug problem, talk to a counselor or medical staff. This can be a good time to quit. A Narcotics Anonymous program is available at most institutions.

...I'm found by C/Os with condoms?

Possession of condoms is an administrative offense. It leads to time added to your sentence. Also, the condoms would be taken away from you.

...or I'm found with bleach or a syringe?

Possession of a syringe is a very serious offense. Stay away from them if you don't want to get into trouble. Possession of bleach, though a less serious offense can also lead to problems.

...I want to use protection during spousal visits?

Pathway to an *Addiction Free* Lifestyle

The CDCR does not provide condoms or any other form of protection to inmates. If you plan to have spousal visits, tell your spouse or partner to bring protection with them.

MYTHS AND FACTS

There are many misconceptions about AIDS, how you can get the HIV virus, and who gets it. False information must be cleared or eliminated, so that people will be more educated about the disease, and won't live in unfounded fear of catching the HIV virus.

Who gets HIV/AIDS?

- AIDS is not a "gay" disease
- AIDS is not a "prostitute" disease
- EVERYBODY CAN GET THE HIV VIRUS

People who are rich and famous get HIV. Suburban housewives get HIV. Teenage kids of all races have gotten HIV. Politicians, rappers and actors, truck drivers and Wall Street people, all get HIV.

HIV/AIDS and TB

- The risk of acquiring tuberculosis is 20 to 37 times greater among HIV-positive individuals

- TB is a leading cause of death among people who are HIV-positive

- About 1/3 of the 33.2 million HIV-positive people worldwide are co-infected with TB and one in four people living with HIV die as a result of TB

HIV/AIDS and HEPATITIS C

- About one quarter of HIV-infected persons in the United States are also infected with Hepatitis C Virus (HCV)

- Co-infection with HIV and HCV is common among HIV-infected injection drug users (IUDs) between 50-90%

HIV does not care about who you are. It doesn't care about your race, color, sexual orientation, features, religion, beliefs, wealth, social status, lifestyle, and job.

HIV cannot be transmitted by animals.

The only place in the world the HIV virus lives in is in the human body (although you may read about the simian immunodeficiency virus — SIV— which is the same kind of virus found in monkeys). HIV cannot survive for long once it comes in contact with the air. In any other living organism, animal or plant, the virus will die.

AIDS cannot be transmitted through casual contact.

HIV is NOT transmitted through hugging, shaking hands, sharing a glass, sharing a plate, using the same toilet, touching the same door handle, sharing a bed, using the same shower, using the same telephone, or wearing the same clothes. Only blood, semen, prejaculate, vaginal secretions and breast milk will transmit the virus, although one may find some of the virus in other bodily fluids. However, these bodily fluids do not have enough "viral load" to result in infection.

AIDS is not transmitted through kissing.

As stated above, the virus is found in saliva, but there are not enough viruses in it to be infectious. There has only been one documented case of anyone being infected with HIV from kissing, and these partners had gum disease. Therefore, there could be a chance in deep kissing, if there is blood present. Still, the chance of this happening is extremely low.

No one has ever gotten HIV through biting.

This is one of the biggest misconceptions. Many people think that if you are bitten by somebody who has HIV or AIDS you will become infected. The chances of that happening are extremely low. In order to transmit HIV through biting, the following circumstances have to occur:

- The bite has to be deep enough to draw blood.

- The other person has to have blood in his or her mouth.

- The blood in the mouth of the attacker has to enter the other person's body.

All of these circumstances are possible, but highly improbable. To this day, no one has ever been infected with HIV through biting.

Mosquitoes and other insects do not transmit the viruses.

As mentioned earlier, HIV can live only inside humans. Even though mosquitoes draw blood from different people at different times, the virus cannot live inside the mosquitoes. The same goes for every other insect. No one has ever been infected with HIV from mosquitoes.

Dentists and physicians do not transmit HIV to patients.

Dentists and physicians will not transmit the virus to their patients. Every person who works in the medical profession takes special precautions to not pass any virus or disease to patients. It is highly unlikely that a medical professional will transmit any virus to patients, much less a virus that is only transmitted through blood and semen.

Rich people do not have cures for AIDS.

The notion that millionaires have "a cure for AIDS" is just plain false. No one has the cure for AIDS. It is true, however, that there are people who have money to get better care and possibly have access to new experimental drugs to slow the progression of the disease.

Pathway to an *Addiction Free* Lifestyle

Frequently Asked Questions

1. **What is HIV? What does HIV stand for? What is AIDS?**

The human immunodeficiency virus (HIV) is a virus, which attacks the immune system, making it difficult for the body to fight off a variety of unusual, and often life threatening diseases. The HIV virus may also cause neuralgic problems such as confusion, memory loss, and difficulty with motor control, and so forth.

At the beginning of the 1980's, the Centers for Disease Control and Prevention (CDC), as the central reporting agency, began getting word of a new illness among gay men that some were calling GRID (Gay-Related Immune Deficiency). As the Agency worked on developing a way for doctors to diagnose this condition, CDC personnel began to notice that similar symptoms were surfacing among addicts who were not necessarily gay. They knew, therefore, that the illness was not, as they had first believed, restricted to the gay community.

As more and more data was collected, it became clear that this condition qualified as a SYNDROME, a condition that causes several other diseases or symptoms. Accordingly, the CDC named it Acquired Immune deficiency Syndrome (AIDS).

2. **How does HIV damage the immune system?**

HIV infects several different cells of the immune system. As more and more cells become infected, there are fewer available to fight off disease. Diseases, which a healthy immune system can overcome, become very powerful and even life threatening for the person with HIV.

3. **Which body fluids contain HIV?**

HIV has been isolated in many different body fluids. CDC recommends precautions are taken with the following fluids:

- Blood
- Semen
- Vaginal secretions
- Breast milk

Other fluids (cerebrospinal fluid, synovial fluid, pleural fluid, peritoneal fluid, amniotic fluid) may contain HIV, but are not transmitted between people except in acute healthcare treatment situations. Menstrual blood would be included in "blood" on this list. It is considered to have a high concentration of virus.

Although HIV has been detected in some of the following fluids, the viral concentrations are not sufficient to cause transmission (unless visible blood is present): tears, saliva, urine, feces, vomit, sputum, nasal secretions. Sweat is not considered a risky fluid.

4. How is HIV transmitted from one person to another? How can it be prevented?

HIV is transmitted in four ways:

1. Unprotected sexual intercourse (anal, vaginal, oral)

2. Sharing of injection drug paraphernalia

3. From an infected woman to her fetus (perinatal transmission) or through her infected breast milk

4. Through direct blood exposure to infected blood through open cuts such as needle sticks (occupational transmission) or through open cuts, sores or other breaks in the skin that would facilitate direct blood-to-blood exposure.

HIV was transmitted through some blood transfusions, and blood products used in treatment of persons with hemophilia before 1985. Since 1985, blood and blood products are carefully screened and treated for HIV. Currently, the risk of HIV transmission through blood transfusions is quite low in the United States.

People can prevent HIV by:

a. Sexual abstinence — don't have sexual intercourse with anyone under any circumstances.

b. Abstinence from injection drug use or other needle sharing activities — NEVER share works.

c. Have sex (sexual intercourse) ONLY with a partner KNOWN not to be infected with HIV.

d. Practice safer sex (which might include mutual masturbation, massage, body rubbing, and use of condoms for all forms of intercourse — anal, vaginal, and oral).

e. Clean injection works with bleach before sharing.

f. Keep a clear head — avoid use of alcohol or other drugs that might impair judgment or resolve to follow safer sex activities.

It is BEHAVIORS which put people at risk for HIV, not membership in any particular "risk group." It is what you do, not who you are!

6. What does it mean when people say that AIDS is not casually transmitted?

A person will not get HIV or AIDS in the normal course of day-to-day contact with family, friends, or coworkers unless that contact involves unprotected sexual intercourse, sharing needles, or other exchanges of blood. Shaking hands, hugging, sharing dishes, showers, bathrooms, telephones, etc. carry NO risk of HIV infection.

Kissing is often a confusing issue. Saliva itself is not a means of HIV transmission, but the mouth may contain sores, lesions, infected areas, or bleeding, and this does suggest a theoretical risk of transmission through deep kissing. Only one such case has ever been documented, and the couple involved both had reported gum disease. For the most part, people are quite safe with kissing unless there are health problems in the mouths of both persons.

What does the term HIV disease mean? What do people mean when they talk about "the spectrum of HIV disease?"

"HIV disease" is a term, which refers to infection with HIV. Any individual who is infected with HIV (that is, anyone who tested positive on the HIV antibody test) can be said to have "HIV disease". This term is now being used commonly in medical settings and in HIV education.

People with HIV disease may have one of several different manifestations of infection. For example, a person can be infected with HIV, have no physical symptoms, and have healthy results on tests of immune function. Or a person can have no physical symptoms but show some signs of immune system damage on medical test of the immune system. A person can also have mild symptoms of HIV disease, or more severe symptoms.

Typically, a person with HIV disease will show an "acute stage" of infection shortly after becoming infected with flu-like symptoms lasting one or two weeks. Then the person will have no physical symptoms for several years. Mild symptoms will develop, and then as time passes, more severe symptoms appear. Actual diagnoses of AIDS are most common at the time that more severe symptoms appear. As of January 1993, a diagnosis of AIDS occurs when an HIV+ person is diagnosed with one or more of the 26 opportunistic infections, or an individual's T4 cell count drops below 200. This is to enable that person to collect health and other financial benefits.

This range of presentations is often called "the spectrum of HIV disease". The phase indicates that there are many possible manifestations of HIV infection.

Many people living with HIV do not like the term "HIV disease", If they are feeling healthy and doing well, they do not believe it is helpful to think of themselves as being "diseased".

HIV infection is not AIDS, and in many cases does not necessarily involve symptoms at all. HIV infection is a range of conditions, from asymptomatic to AIDS.

Pathway to an *Addiction Free* Lifestyle

Following is a graphic representation of the spectrum of HIV infection from asymptomatic to AIDS:

HIGH RISK BEHAVIOR ⟶ INCUBATION PERIOD ⟶ SYMPTOMATIC

Exposure / Infection	Antibody Positive (Seroconversion) Infection Window Period - Average: 2-12 weeks (1-15+ years)	Healthy HIV + Asymptomatic	Pre-AIDS Symptomatic	AIDS Or HIV Disease

Can mosquitoes transmit HIV or AIDS?

Extensive laboratory and epidemiological studies in Belle Glade, Florida and Africa have clearly demonstrated that mosquitoes and other biting insects do not transmit HIV. The cells of fruit flies, ticks, moths and mosquitoes have been examined and none have shown HIV replication. Laboratory experiments were conducted to determine if mosquitoes and bedbugs could transmit HIV from infected blood to non-infected blood through a membrane. No transmission of virus occurred with mosquitoes or bedbugs. HIV does not establish productive infection in insects and therefore cannot be transmitted to humans they bite. In other words, they can't utilize the virus, so they don't pass it on. The volume of blood on a mosquito's mouthparts is 100 times smaller than the volume of blood that would be transmitted in the case of a needle stick injury. The risk of HIV infection from a needle stick injury is less than one percent.

When a mosquito bites someone, it injects a tiny bit of anti-coagulant into the person to make the blood flow more easily. It does not inject blood from other people it has bitten.

Mosquitoes are able to transmit malaria because the malaria organism actually uses the mosquito as part of its life cycle. In order to be able to reproduce, it has to spend time in a mosquito's body. However, HIV cannot survive in mosquito cells.

Scientists fed HIV-infected blood to a mosquito. Then, they immediately killed the mosquito and opened it up — of course, the blood was still there and the HIV was still in the blood. When they waited even a few minutes before killing the mosquito, the mosquito digested the blood and the HIV could no longer be found. This is how we know that HIV cannot live in mosquitoes.

Studies have been done where swarms of mosquitoes were given a tray of HIV infected blood. Scientist interrupted them mid-feeding and transferred them to a tray of uninfected blood, where they resumed feeding.

Then, scientists tested the uninfected blood, to see whether the mosquitoes had transmitted the virus. Despite repeated tests, no HIV could be found.

The final proof that mosquitoes are not spreading HIV is circumstantial. Everybody knows that children who play outside all summer long get many mosquito bites. If mosquitoes could spread HIV, we would be seeing many more children with HIV, especially in places where there is a high population with AIDS, and this is not happening.

8. Where can I get an HIV test? How long after exposure to HIV does it take for the antibody test to turn positive? How does the test work? What does the term "antibody" really mean?

Outside prison, you can go to an anonymous testing center. You can also request an HIV antibody test through your private physician or your HMO. Within prison, you can submit a CDC 7362 Medical Form.

A person will test antibody positive anywhere from two to 12 weeks after high-risk behavior transmission has occurred. When you get a blood test for HIV, the technicians are NOT searching for the HIV virus, but for antibodies to the virus. That is why a doctor might tell patients who think they have been exposed to wait for a time before being tested. If your body is producing antibodies to HIV, or your test indicates you are HIV positive (HIV+), you have been infected.

Antibodies are cells designed to neutralize invading viruses or the many other foreign biological substances that enter the system. Antibodies are custom-designed to match the invader's structure.

9. Why does a person die from AIDS and how long does it take?

People don't die from AIDS per se, but from opportunistic infections that their bodies cannot protect them against. That's because the HIV virus suppresses their immune systems. There are many variables concerning how long an individual can live after he or she has been diagnosed as having AIDS. Even with a suppressed immune system, an individual can live a very long time, and live a productive and positive life. Factors such as stress reduction, good nutrition, emotional support, exercise, prophylactics and treatment, etc. can contribute to the quality and length of life.

10. Does anyone ever survive AIDS?

It depends on the definition of "survive". There are people alive who have had HIV for many years. In 1988, the New York Daily News printed an article in its magazine section called "Why Do Some People Survive AIDS?" This article followed people who had lived three years or more. Michael Callen wrote a book, "Surviving AIDS". His criteria were people who had survived an AIDS diagnosis for three years or more.

Those people tend to be realistic, willing to take responsibility for their own healing, have extraordinary relationships with their health-care providers, are passionately committed to living, have faced and overcome past life crises, and are assertive and able to communicate openly.

11. Why can't AIDS be cured like other STDs?

HIV is a retrovirus, unlike many other viruses. It lives and reproduces in the immune system, the very system that is supposed to fight off infections. Therefore, once it is inside the human immune system, it cannot be "cured" or removed.

12. What is the life expectancy of a person with AIDS?

No one knows. A person diagnosed with AIDS can die within a year, or live many years - so as of now, there is no way to say.

13. What are T cells or T4 cells?

T4 cells (or CD4 cells, or helper cells - the terms are interchangeable - often referred to imply as T cells) are cells that moderate the body's response to infection. The T4 cells determine, on the basis of the invader's structure, what an antibody should look like. Also, T4 cells "remember" every biological invader that ever entered the system and can respond immediately if the body has fought the particular invader before. So, if you had measles as a child, your T4 cells will respond to an invading measles virus by "recalling" the antibodies the body made for measles and produce new ones within hours.

14. How reliable are condoms? What kind? Should spermicides be used?

Condoms alone do no equate to safer sex. They must be used correctly and consistently to ensure safety. Used correctly, latex condoms are one of the most effective ways to protect yourself and your partner from sexually transmitted diseases (STDs), including AIDS. Condoms protect you by preventing contact with body fluids - such as semen, blood, and vaginal fluids - that could be carrying the virus that causes AIDS.

Condom manufactures say that there are several things that can weaken a condom, such as prolonged exposure to heat and light. They shouldn't be kept in a wallet or glove compartment for very long for this reason. Many condoms are dated and should be used before the date expires. If lubricants are used, they should be water based, as oil based lubricants, such as Vaseline, cold cream, hand lotion or baby oil, weakens the latex.

Condoms must be used consistently and correctly to provide maximum protection. Consistent use means using a condom from start to finish with each act of intercourse.

Correct condom use should include the following steps:

   a. Use a new condom for each act of intercourse.

   b. Put on the condom as soon as erection occurs and before any sexual contact (anal, vaginal or oral).

   c. Hold the tip of the condom and unroll it onto the erect penis, leaving space at the tip of the condom, yet ensuring that no air is trapped in the condoms tip.

d. Withdraw from the partner immediately after ejaculation, holding the condom firmly to keep it from slipping off.

A commonly held misperception is that latex condoms contain "holes" that allow passage of HIV. Although this may be true for natural membrane condoms, laboratory studies show that intact latex condoms provide a continuous barrier for microorganisms, including HIV, as well as sperm.

A condom for women - received approval from the federal government. Women who like the device include:

  a. Women who are ready to stop using birth control pills and want to try a barrier method;

  b. Women who are allergic to latex, but want to use a barrier method;

  c. Women who want the option of using both a male condom and female condom so each partner is sharing the responsibility for protection against disease and pregnancy.

Another advantage of the pouch is that it is not disruptive to sex because a woman can insert it minutes or hours before intercourse. Like the male condom, the female condom can only be used once.

15. How reliable is the blood test for HIV?

When a HIV test is taken, a small amount of blood is drawn from the arm. The blood is then taken to a laboratory and tested.

There are two HIV tests that are given. The ELISA test, which stands for enzyme-linked Immunosorbent assay, is the test used at clinics, hospitals, and counseling and testing centers.

The ELISA test looks for the presence of antibodies that your body might have developed to fight HIV. When someone becomes infected with HIV, antibodies to the virus are produced, usually within two to six months, after exposure to HIV.

A positive ELISA test might not mean you are infected with HIV, but it would be a sign that further testing is needed. If you test positive for HIV antibodies with an ELISA test, a confirmatory test should be performed automatically.

Confirmatory tests are more specific than ELISA tests. Laboratories are instructed not to release positive test results until confirmatory tests have been conducted. Confirmatory tests are designed to identity false-positive test results. ELISA tests are considered to 99% accurate, but some false positive results occur.

If you test negative for HIV infection, a confirmatory test will not be performed. However, you can not be sure that you are not infected with the virus if you have recently engaged in risky behavior. Your body might not have had time to develop antibodies to HIV. If you have engaged in high-risk activities such as having unprotected sex and sharing needles during the previous six months, you should be tested again a few months later.

If you test positive, the CDC says you must contact your sexual partners and tell them about the infection. You must also understand that you can infect other people through sexual contact and sharing needles and syringes. You can also infect your unborn child.

Testing positive for HIV antibodies does not mean you already have AIDS. It can take years for you to develop symptoms of AIDS, particularly since treatments are available to help people infected with HIV stay well longer. People infected with HIV should get medical care as soon as possible.

16. How did AIDS get started and how did it get here?

No one really knows — however, there are a number of theories. Some scientists believe that AIDS started in the green monkeys in Africa, and then somehow got into the human population, maybe through monkey bites. Once it got into humans, it was spread through sex and shared needles, and then traveled from Africa to Haiti to the US via tourists and other travelers.

On the other hand, some people believe the virus might have been created in a laboratory, as part of germ warfare research. Some people think the Pentagon or CIA created the virus. And some scientists have found evidence which they believe supports the theory that HIV actually originated in the US and then spread to Africa via American tourists who visited Haiti. Once again, no one really knows.

The important thing is not where AIDS came from, but the fact that it's here, now, and we have to deal with it. AIDS is not the first killer epidemic; there have been plagues throughout history. Societies have survived these plagues by learning what they had to do to protect themselves, and doing_ it, while also providing compassionate care to the sick.

NOTE: There is some controversy surrounding this question, because some people believe the theory of an African AIDS origin is racist, or that teaching the theory permits or encourages "blaming" Black people for AIDS. It is important to be sensitive to this issue, handle "The Origin" question in a non-judgmental way, and move on to other, more pertinent questions as quickly as possible.

17. What is "high risk" behavior? Are there "high risk" groups?

High-risk behavior is any activity that would allow the HIV virus to enter the body. These behaviors include unprotected sexual intercourse (anal, vaginal and oral), sharing drug works including needles or syringes. There are no "high risk" groups, only "high risk" activities. In other words, its not who you do, it's what you do.

18. Can people of all ages get HIV?

Yes, Adolescents and adults of all ages can become infected through high-risk behavior.

19. If you want to have sex with someone, how will you know if she or he has HIV?

You can only be sure if your potential partner tests negative for HIV antibodies after six months of practicing no risk activities. You can be safe in the meantime if you use latex condoms every time you have intercourse.

20. If you have sex with someone who has AIDS, is it 100% sure you will get the disease if you do not use protection?

No. Some people exposed to HIV do not become infected. It's impossible to predict if that will occur. Being tested six weeks after high-risk behavior and again in six months with negative results would indicate that you were most likely not infected. Having unprotected sex with someone who has HIV or AIDS is considered VERY high-risk behavior.

21. What is "safe sex"? What is "safer sex"?

Safe sex is abstinence form sexual intercourse. There are other forms of making love, such as mutual masturbation, body rubbing, massage, etc. that would be considered "safe sex". Protected intercourse, whether vaginal, oral or anal, is "safer sex". This involves using a condom correctly, consistently, and when using lubrication, choosing a water-based product.

22. If you can get HIV when the virus enters the bloodstream, does the semen enter the bloodstream during intercourse? How else can you get HIV when you have sexual intercourse with someone who has HIV?

HIV can enter the bloodstream during intercourse in several ways. It can enter through the vaginal wall, through the lining of the rectum, through a cut in the mouth, and through an open cut on the penis.

23. Will AIDS take over the world?

No, although it is an epidemic, there have been other epidemics and plagues throughout history, and they haven't taken over the world. HIV has not spread to most countries throughout the world, however.

24. Was AIDS caused by homosexuals?

No. AIDS is spread through unprotected sex and sharing IV needles. So, once it gets into a particular community, it spreads between whoever is doing those things. Gay men were among the first people in this country to get the virus; then they had sex with other gay men, or in some cases shared needles with other gay men. Now AIDS is spreading rapidly among drug users for the same reason. But all along, people who did not fall into these "risk groups" have also gotten AIDS: hemophiliacs, infants and sexual partners of infected people. That's why we no longer talk about "risk groups"; instead, we talk about risk behaviors, such as unprotected sex.

25. How should people with HIV be treated?

They should be treated with kindness and compassion. Since HIV cannot be transmitted through casual contact, there is no danger in hugging, kissing, or in any other casual way being physical with someone who has HIV or AIDS. A person with AIDS has a suppressed immune system and may have opportunistic infections associated with that condition. This person needs and is entitled to the same love, care, kindness, and respect that we all want.

Say you've been exposed to the virus, either by a needle in your arm, or unsafe sex; can all your blood be taken out of your body right away and exchanged so you won't be infected?

No, if you've been exposed, you may not necessarily become infected, but it's too late to do anything to prevent infection at that point. There is no "morning after" pill or treatment for HIV infection. Antibody testing after six weeks and again at six months might give conclusive proof as to whether or not you have been infected.

26. What about oral sex?

HIV can be transmitted through oral sex if there is an open sore in the mouth of the person performing oral sex on the partner, or if either partner has an open sore on the penis or in the vagina. As long as there is the possibility of vaginal fluid or semen containing HIV entering another person's bloodstream, there is the possibility of infection. Since gums tend to bleed after flossing, and sometimes brushing, it would be advisable NOT to floss or brush before engaging in oral sex.

27. Can you get HIV from public swimming pools or hot tubs?

No. HIV does not live in water and cannot multiply in water. Theoretically, HIV might be present in untreated sewage or water, which is contaminated with human waste or blood. Contact with such water has always been risky for reasons other than the more recent threat of HIV transmission.

The possible risk of HIV infection from swimming pools and hot tubs has been a concern. Many will remember the polio epidemic in the 1950s where a number of swimming pools were closed for fear that a person could become infected with the polio virus through water. Polio differs from HIV in that polio is transmitted through contact with infected saliva, mucus and feces, but even transmission of polio by water is a rare occurrence. HIV is transmitted through sexual contact and blood, not through casual contact in or out of the water.

28. How can needles and syringes be cleaned?

The recommendations (when no other safer options are available, CDC Newsletter, August 1993) for disinfecting needles and syringes are summarized as follows:

- Needles and syringes should be filled and washed out several times with cledn water before disinfecting with bleach.

- After washing with water, full-strength, undiluted bleach should be used for the needle and syringe for at least 30 seconds.

- Needles and syringes should then be rinsed with clean water. Water that was used for the first wash must not be-re-used for this rinse, as it may be contaminated.

- Fill the syringe completely ("to the-top") every time it is rinsed with water or cleaned with bleach. Shaking and tapping the syringe are recommended each time the syringe is filled to improve the effectiveness of each step.

Pathway to an *Addiction Free* Lifestyle

- Taking the syringe apart by removing the plunger and soaking both pieces in bleach may improve the cleaning or disinfecting of parts.

- Also remember: never share cookers, cottons, rinse water, bleach, or any other paraphernalia (equipment/works).

Following all of these steps will provide the greatest potential for reducing the risk of HIV transmission from reused needles and syringes. However, for those who cannot do so, performing as many of these steps as possible is the next best option.

Pathway to an *Addiction Free* Lifestyle

Pathway to an Addiction Free Lifestyle

OPPORTUNISTIC INFECTION FACT SHEET

Candidiasis (Thrush): Thrush is a fungal infection of the mouth and throat, which results in whitish patches on the tongue, gums or throat lining. Swallowing and eating is painful, and often results in a loss of appetite.

Cryptococcosis: Cryptococcosis is a fungal infection which results in fevers, nausea, flu-like symptoms, loss of appetite and, commonly, meningitis (inflammation of the tissue surrounding the brain), which can create headaches and changes in personality.

Cryptosporidiosis (Crypto): Crypto is a parasitic infection commonly found in drinking water. Crypto results in diarrhea, stomach cramps, loss of appetite, vomiting, dehydration and constipation.

Cytomegalovirus (CMV): CMV is a virus, which can affect the eyes, throat or colon. CMV can lead to blurred vision, blindness, difficulty swallowing, stomach pain and diarrhea.

Herpes Simplex Virus (HSV/Shingles): Herpes Simplex can result in painful. itchy blisters on the lips (HSV-1) or the genitals and anal area (HSV-2). Shingles (Herpes Zoster) is a chicken pox infection, which usually is found on the legs or chest area.

Pneumocystis Carinii Pneumonia (PCP): PCP is a lung infection, which causes tremendous difficulty for breathing and the respiratory system. Systems are fatigue, fever, a dry cough, shortness of breath, flu-like feeling, weight loss and night sweats.

Mycobacterium Avium Complex (MAC): MAC is a bacterial infection which causes fever, weight loss, night sweats, chronic diarrhea, weakness, dizziness, stomach pain and swollen lymph glands. MAC can be located in a particular body organ or spread throughout the body.

Toxoplasmosis (Toxo): Toxo is a parasitic infection which usually affects the brain and can cause paralysis on one side of the body, personality changes, numbness, delusions, imbalance, severe headaches, muscle spasms, seizures, fever and comas.

Tuberculosis (TB): TB is a bacterial infection with symptoms similar to MAC. TB typically isolates in the lungs.

Pathway to an *Addiction Free* Lifestyle

Pathway to an *Addiction Free* Lifestyle

HIV/AIDS TEST

1. HIV is the same thing as AIDS.

    A. True

    B. False

2. The safest way of protecting against the spread of the HIV virus is:

    A. Latex condom

    B. Dental Dam

    C. Abstinence

    D. Both A & B

3. The most common test used to check for the presence of the HIV virus in humans is the :

    A. Factor Eight Blood Test

    B. Anatomical Body Fluid Test

    C. Western Blot

    D. Elisa Test

4. HIV is found in the greatest amounts in blood.

    A. True

    B. False

5. What body system does HIV attack and weaken, allowing other infections to occur:

    A. Immune System

    B. Respiratory System

    C. Reproductive System

6. HIV risk factors do not include blood transfusions.

    A. True

    B. False

7. Which of the following activities poses the highest risk of transmitting the HIV virus to another human?

A. A mosquito bite

B. Hugging an infected person

C. Breathing in a closed room with an HIV infected person

D. Having someone give you a tattoo

8. Which of the following symptoms is not normally consistent with HIV infection:

    A. Fever lasting more than 10 days

    B. Hair loss

    C. Severe night sweats

    D. Tumor (Kaposi's Sarcoma)

9. If a person with HIV also has an STD:

    A. Medical evaluation is important because untreated STD's are serious health threats to HIV infected individuals.

    B. Should start medical treatment for HIV; these medications will also cure to treat STDs

    C. Additional medication for STDs should be avoided because they can cause further deterioration of the person's immune system

    D. STD's are a minor consideration compared to the patient's more troublesome HIV condition

10. Which of the following human body fluids of an HIV infected person would be the least likely to transmit HIV virus to another adult human?

    A. Blood

    B. Sperm

    C. Vaginal fluids

    D. Saliva

    E. Medicine

Answers:

1) B 2) C 3) D 4) A 5) A 6) A 7) D 8) B 9) A 10) D

BOTULISM

CHARLES PATRICK DAVIS, MD, PhD

Dr. Charles "Pat" Davis, MD, PhD, is a board certified Emergency Medicine doctor who currently practices as a consultant and staff member for hospitals. He has a PhD in Microbiology (UT at Austin), and the MD (Univ. Texas Medical Branch, Galveston). He is a Clinical Professor (retired) in the Division of Emergency Medicine, UT Health Science Center at San Antonio, and has been the Chief of Emergency Medicine at UT Medical Branch and at UTHSCSA with over 250 publications.

Dr. Davis obtained a BS degree from St. Edward's University and a PhD in microbiology from the University of Texas, both in Austin, Texas. He completed his MD and residency training in Internal Medicine at the University of Texas Medical Branch (UTMB) in Galveston, Texas. He has served as an editor and chapter author for several medical textbooks. He has been the supervising professor for several successful PhD candidates in Microbiology, established a Master's degree for physicians at UTMB and was the supervising professor for its first graduate and is a consultant in Microbiology.

Dr. Davis lives in San Antonio, Texas, with his wife Barbara. They share hobbies of water activities, snow skiing, fishing (especially eating the catch!), traveling, and reading; they plan to continue these activities with their son, Drew, his wife, Amber and the new family addition, grandson Cy.

MELISSA CONRAD STÖPPLER, MD

Melissa Conrad Stöppler, MD, is a U.S. board-certified anatomic pathologist with subspecialty training in the fields of experimental and molecular pathology. Dr. Stöppler's educational background includes a BA with highest distinction from the University of Virginia and an MD from the University of North Carolina. She completed residency training in anatomic pathology at Georgetown University followed by subspecialty fellowship training in molecular diagnostics and experimental pathology.

Dr. Stöppler served as an assistant professor of pathology in the Georgetown University School of Medicine and has also served on the medical faculty at the University of Marburg, Germany. Her research in the area of virus-induced cancers has been funded by the National Institutes of Health as well as by private foundations. She has a broad list of medical publications, abstracts, and posters and has taught medical students and residents both in the United States and Germany. Dr. Stöppler was named a fellow of the Alexander von Humboldt Society in Germany and was a recipient of a Physician Scientist Award from the U.S. National Cancer Institute.

An active medical journalist and writer, Dr. Stöppler currently serves on the medical editorial board of MedicineNet.com and is the chief medical editor of eMedicineHealth.com, both WebMD Inc. companies. Her experience also includes translation and editing of medical texts in German and English. Dr. Stöppler's special interests in medicine include family health and fitness, patient education/empowerment, and molecular diagnostic pathology.

Pathway to an *Addiction Free* Lifestyle

Dr. Stöppler is currently a specialist consultant in the breast oncology research program at the University of California, San Francisco School of Medicine and is co-editor-in-chief of *Webster's New World Medical Dictionary*, Year 2008 Third Edition.

She currently resides in the San Francisco Bay area with her husband and their three children.

What is botulism?

Botulism is a serious illness that causes flaccid paralysis of muscles. It is caused by a neurotoxin, generically called botulinum toxin, produced by the bacterium *Clostridium botulinum* (and rarely by *C. butyricum* and *C. baratii*). There are seven distinct neurotoxins (types A-G) that *Clostridium botulinum* produces, but types A, B, and E (and rarely F) are the most common that produce the flaccid paralysis in humans. The other types mainly cause disease in animals and birds, which also develop flaccid paralysis. Most *Clostridium* species produce only one type of neurotoxin; however, the effects of A, B, E, or F on humans are essentially the same. Botulism is not transmitted from person to person. Botulism develops if a person ingests the toxin (or rarely, if it is inhaled or injected) or if the *Clostridium* spp. organisms grow in the intestines or wounds in the body and toxin is released.

The recorded history of botulism begins in 1735, when the disease was first associated with German sausage (food-borne disease or food poisoning after eating sausage). In 1870, a German physician by the name of Muller derived the name botulism from the Latin word for sausage. *Clostridium botulinum* bacteria were first isolated in 1895, and a neurotoxin that it produces was isolated in 1944 by Dr. Edward Schantz. From 1949 to the 1950s, the toxin (named BoNT A) was shown to block neuromuscular transmissions by blocking the release of acetylcholine from motor nerve endings. Botulism toxin(s) are some of the most toxic substances known to man; while the toxin has been considered for use as a biological weapon, it has also been used to treat many medical conditions. In 1980, Dr. Scott used the toxin to treat strabismus (deviation of the eye), and in December 1989, BoNT-A (BOTOX) was approved by the U.S. Food and Drug Administration (FDA) for the treatment of strabismus, blepharospasm, and hemifacial spasm in young patients. The use of BOTOX to treat glabellar lines (wrinkles and frown lines) was approved in 2002 by the FDA for cosmetic improvements; the FDA has approved many additional uses (for example, underarm sweating, and muscle pain disorders) since 2002.

What causes botulism?

Neurotoxin, synthesized and secreted by *Clostridium botulinum* bacteria (and a few other *Clostridium* species), cause botulism. The toxin causes the disease by blocking the release of acetylcholine from motor nerve endings. This result produces the symptoms associated with botulism.

How many kinds of botulism are there?

There are three main kinds of botulism, which are categorized by the way in which the disease is acquired:

- **Food-borne botulism** is caused by eating foods that contain the botulinum neurotoxin. Recent small outbreaks have occurred in Canada due to fermented fish and in New York due to unrefrigerated bulk tofu contamination.
- **Wound botulism** is caused by neurotoxin produced from a wound that is infected with the bacteria *Clostridium botulinum*.
- **Infant botulism** occurs when an infant consumes the spores of the botulinum bacteria. The bacteria then grow in the intestines and release the neurotoxin.

Three other kinds of botulism have been described but are seen rarely. The first is adult intestinal colonization that is seen in older children and adults with abnormal bowels. Only rarely does intestinal infection with *Clostridium botulinum* bacteria occur in adults. Typically, the adult form of this intestinal botulism is related to abdominal surgical procedures. The second kind (injection botulism) is seen in patients injected with inappropriately high amounts of therapeutic neurotoxin (for example, BOTOX, Dysport, Myobloc), while the third kind (inhalation botulism) has occurred in laboratory personnel who work with the neurotoxins. All six kinds of botulism are potentially fatal.

How serious is botulism?

Botulinum neurotoxin is considered one of the most potent, lethal substances known. As little as about 1 nanogram/kg can be lethal to an individual, and scientists have estimated that about 1 gram could potentially kill 1 million people. This small amount of toxin capable of killing humans has made the toxin a candidate for use in weapons for biowarfare and bioterrorism. All forms of botulism can be fatal and are considered medical emergencies. Food-borne botulism can be especially dangerous because many people can be poisoned by eating even small amounts of neurotoxin-contaminated food. A botulism outbreak is a public-health emergency that is reportable to the U.S. government.

How does botulism neurotoxin affect the body?

A neurotoxin actually paralyzes the nerves so that the muscles cannot contract. This happens when the neurotoxin enters nerve cells and eventually interferes with the release of acetylcholine so the nerve cannot stimulate the muscle to contract. Unless the nerve can regenerate a new axon that has no exposure to the neurotoxin, the interference at the neuromuscular junction is permanent. This is why it takes so long to recover from botulism and also why cosmetic and therapeutic uses of diluted neurotoxin can be effective for relatively lengthy time periods.

What kind of organism is *Clostridium botulinum*?

Clostridium botulinum is the name of bacteria commonly found in soil all over the world. The bacteria are considered to be anaerobic, which means these organisms grow best in low or absent oxygen levels. *Clostridium* bacteria are gram-positive rod-shaped bacteria that form spores that allow the bacteria to survive in a dormant state until exposed to conditions that can support growth. There are seven types of botulism neurotoxin designated by the letters A through G. Only types A, B, E, and F cause illness in humans.

How common is botulism?

Because of better canning processes, especially with home canning or home processing of food, the number of yearly cases has dropped to about 1,000 worldwide. In the United States, on average, 110 cases of botulism are reported each year. Of these, nearly 25% of cases are food-borne, approximately 72% are infant botulism, and the remainder (about 3%) are wound botulism, which until recently was rare. Outbreaks of food-borne botulism involving two or more people are usually caused by eating contaminated home-canned foods. The number of cases of food-borne and infant botulism has changed little in recent years. However, the incidence of wound botulism has increased, especially in California, from the use of black-tar heroin, which causes infected wounds at heroin injection sites.

What are botulism symptoms and signs?

The classic symptoms of botulism include double vision, blurred vision, drooping eyelids, slurred speech, difficulty swallowing, dry mouth, and muscle weakness. Constipation may occur. The doctor's examination may reveal that the gag reflex and the deep tendon reflexes like the knee-jerk reflex are decreased or absent.

Infants with botulism appear lethargic, weak, and floppy, feed poorly, become constipated, and have a weak cry and poor muscle tone. In infants, constipation is often the first symptom to occur.

These are all symptoms of the muscle paralysis that is caused by the bacterial neurotoxin. If untreated, these symptoms may progress to cause paralysis in various parts of the body, often seen as a descending paralysis of the arms, legs, trunk, and breathing muscles.

How soon do symptoms appear?

In food-borne botulism, symptoms generally begin 18-36 hours after eating a contaminated food, but they can occur as early as six hours or as late as 10 days afterward.

How is botulism diagnosed?

The patient's history and physical examination may suggest botulism, but these clues are usually not enough to allow a diagnosis of botulism. Symptoms of other diseases, such as a stroke, Guillain-Barré syndrome (another disease of muscle paralysis), and myasthenia gravis (which also causes weakness and eyelid drooping) can appear similar to those of botulism. Special tests may be needed to exclude these other conditions. These tests may include a brain scan, spinal fluid examination, nerve conduction test (electromyography, or EMG), and a tensilon test for myasthenia gravis. However, if botulism is strongly suspected (for example, several patients with botulism symptoms who ate from the same home-preserved food container), samples should be obtained for a mouse inoculation test (see below) and then the patients should be treated immediately with botulism antiserum. These tests will help distinguish botulism from infections with *Salmonella*, *E. coli*, and other *Clostridium* species (tetanus).

The most direct way to confirm the diagnosis is to identify the botulinum neurotoxin in the patient's blood, serum, or stool. This is done by injecting the patient's serum or stool into the peritoneal cavity of mice. An equal amount of serum or stool from the patient is treated with multivalent antitoxin and injected in other mice. If the antitoxin-treated serum- or stool-injected mice live while those injected with untreated serum or stool die, then this is a positive test for botulism and is called the mouse inoculation test. The bacteria can also be isolated from the stool of people with food-borne and infant botulism, but this is not a definitive test. However, stool cultures can help differentiate botulism from *E. coli*, *Salmonella*, and other infectious agents.

How is botulism treated?

If diagnosed early, food-borne and wound botulism can be treated with an antitoxin that blocks the action of neurotoxin circulating in the blood. The trivalent antitoxin (effective against three neurotoxins: A, B, and E) is dispensed from quarantine stations by the U.S. government's Centers for Disease Control and Prevention (CDC). The antitoxin can prevent the disorder from worsening, but recovery still takes many weeks. Another heptavalent antitoxin (effective against seven neurotoxins: A, B, C, D, E, F, and G) may be available from the U.S. Army or FEMA. Physicians may remove whatever contaminated food is still in the gut by inducing vomiting or by using enemas. Wounds should be treated, usually surgically, to remove the source of the toxin-producing bacteria. Good supportive care in a hospital is the mainstay of therapy for all kinds of botulism.

Antitoxin is not routinely given for the treatment of infant botulism; however, a new product that recently became available from the orphan drug program can be used to treat botulism in infants. The product is comprised of immune globulins that can be given intravenously to infants who have been diagnosed with infant botulism. The new treatment is named BabyBIG (Botulism Immune Globulin, given IV) and is only currently available from a special site. Call 510-231-7600 for specific information about this treatment.

The respiratory failure and paralysis that occur with severe botulism may require a patient to be on a breathing machine (ventilator) for weeks and may require intensive medical and nursing care. After several weeks, the paralysis slowly improves as axons in the nerves are regenerated.

What are complications from botulism?

Botulism can result in death from respiratory failure. However, in the past 50 years, the rate of death from botulism has fallen from about 60% to 8%. Unfortunately, to survive, a patient with severe botulism may require not only a breathing machine but also intensive medical and nursing care for several months.

Patients who survive an episode of botulism poisoning may experience fatigue and shortness of breath for years, and long-term therapy may be needed to aid recovery.

In 2009, the FDA increased its label precautions on the three available products: BOTOX, Dysport, and Myobloc. All three are different formulations of the toxin and are not interchangeable with regard to dosing. In addition, the FDA cautions that all the symptoms of botulism can occur if the treatments are inappropriately given, especially in high doses or if some of the solution seeps out of the localized area where it is injected. The FDA further warned care providers that suppliers of medical toxins that do not have FDA approval may supply faulty products that could harm individuals.

What is the prognosis (outcome) of people with botulism?

Untreated botulism has a mortality rate (death rate) of about 50%. Appropriately treated patients with botulism currently still have a mortality rate of about 3%-5%. Some patients may experience various degrees of paralysis for many months. In general, the earlier the diagnosis and treatment of the disease, the better is the prognosis. However, outcomes may be considered only fair in some patients who develop chronic fatigue and shortness of breath for many years after the initial diagnosis and treatment of botulism.

Can botulism be prevented?

Yes. Food-borne botulism has often come from improperly prepared home-canned foods such as asparagus, green beans, beets, and corn. However, there have been outbreaks of botulism from more unusual sources such as chopped garlic in oil, agave nectar, chili peppers, broccoli, tomatoes, tomato sauce, improperly handled baked potatoes wrapped in aluminum foil, and home-canned or fermented fish. People who do home canning should follow strict hygienic procedures to prevent or kill *Clostridium* bacteria, their spores, and neutralize its neurotoxin. Oils that are infused with garlic or herbs should be refrigerated. Potatoes that have been baked while wrapped in aluminum foil should be kept hot until served or refrigerated. Bacon should be cooked well since bacon preservatives (salts), which inhibit clostridial spores, have been reduced. Because botulism neurotoxin is destroyed by high temperatures (85 C for five minutes), people who eat home-canned foods should consider boiling the food for 10 minutes before eating it to help ensure that the food is safe to consume. Bulging cans or abnormal-smelling preserved foods should be discarded. Do not taste-test them or attempt to boil the food!

Because honey can contain spores of *Clostridium botulinum* and this has been a source of infection for infants, children less than 12 months old should not be fed honey. Honey is relatively safe for people 1 year of age and older.

Wound botulism can be prevented by promptly seeking medical care for infected wounds or skin cuts and avoiding injectable street drugs.

The FDA publishes recall lists of commercially produced foods that may contain botulinum toxin. The most recent large recall was Castleberry Food Company's hot dog chili sauces and dog food in 2007. In October 2009, Plumb Organics issued a recall of baby food (apple and carrot preparations) that may be tainted with botulinum toxin. Avoiding such potential sources of toxin can prevent botulism.

Vaccine development for the major human types of botulism neurotoxin is currently being investigated, but there is no vaccine commercially available or approved for public use by the FDA. However, in the United States, an investigational pentavalent (against neurotoxins A, B, C, D, and E) botulinum toxoid vaccine can be distributed by the CDC for laboratory workers at high risk of exposure to botulinum toxin and by the military for protection of troops against attack. Unfortunately, it takes several months to induce immunity. In 2009, a new research finding with molecules that mimic botulism toxin binding sites may provide another method to block toxin from binding to nerve tissues, but this approach is only in the research phase of development.

The herb milk thistle has been suggested by alternative medicine proponents (mainly in Europe) to treat food poisoning (especially mushroom poisoning) and to help detoxify the liver. There is no good data on its use in preventing or treating botulism.

Is botulism neurotoxin really considered to be a potential biological weapon?

Yes. However, the neurotoxin rapidly inactivates when exposed to air and is relatively unstable even in liquid formulations in contrast to other disease agents like organisms that cause anthrax. Even with these drawbacks, the neurotoxin has been used sporadically in attempts to harm or kill individuals. Botulinum toxin could be used to contaminate food supplies, but some experts suggest that dissemination of the toxin as an aerosol would be more effective. During the Gulf War, Iraq reportedly produced 20,000 L of botulinum toxin and used 12,000 L for field-testing and to fill warheads, but the shells were not used. The Aum Shinrikyo cult in Japan tried and failed three times to use the toxin as an aerosol weapon. Scientists in Russia also have experimented with botulinum toxin as a weapon. These situations are described in detail in the literature that discusses chemical and biological warfare.

Why are botulism neurotoxins used as cosmetic treatments or treatments for some medical conditions?

Interestingly, purified and highly diluted botulism toxin is being used to treat conditions that are characterized by abnormal muscle contractions. (Some examples of these conditions are torticollis, spasmodic dysphonia, achalasia, strabismus, oromandibular dystonia, cervical dystonia, and blepharospasm.)

Wrinkles are caused by repeated normal muscle contractions...no muscle contractions, no wrinkles. Consequently, many people elect to have an FDA-approved formulation of the dilute toxin injected to reduce or stop wrinkles in the skin. This wrinkle treatment was first approved by the FDA in 2002. Possible side effects of this treatment include bruising, ptosis (abnormal drooping of a body part, especially the eyelid), nausea, and dysphasia (difficulty with speech), but other side effects may also occur. The last reference listed below shows pictures of frown line treatment with BOTOX.

REFERENCES:

Infant Botulism Treatment and Prevention Program. <http://www.infantbotulism.org/>.

Kedlaya, Divakara. "Botulinum Toxin." Medscape.com. Apr. 25, 2012.
<http://emedicine.medscape.com/article/325451-overview>.

Patel, Bhupendra. "Ophthalmologic Manifestations of Botulism." Feb. 15, 2012.
<http://emedicine.medscape.com/article/1203301-overview>.

Schlessinger, Joel. "Botox Injections." eMedicineHealth.com. July 17, 2012.
<http://www.emedicinehealth.com/botox_injections/article_em.htm>.

United States. Centers for Disease Control and Prevention. "Botulism." May 21, 2008.
<http://www.cdc.gov/nczved/dfbmd/disease_listing/botulism_gi.html>.

Pathway to an *Addiction Free* Lifestyle

United States. Centers for Disease Control and Prevention. "Facts About Botulism." Oct. 6, 2006. <http://www.bt.cdc.gov/agent/botulism/factsheet.asp>.

Wenhma, Tim, and Andrew Cohen. "Botulism." Medscape. June 27, 2008. <http://www.medscape.com/viewarticle/574270_3>.

Pathway to an *Addiction Free* Lifestyle

Information from CDC
Facts about Botulism

Botulism is a muscle-paralyzing disease caused by a toxin made by a bacterium called *Clostridium botulinum*.

There are three main kinds of botulism:

- Foodborne botulism occurs when a person ingests pre-formed toxin that leads to illness within a few hours to days. Foodborne botulism is a public health emergency because the contaminated food may still be available to other persons besides the patient.
- Infant botulism occurs in a small number of susceptible infants each year who harbor *C. botulinum* in their intestinal tract.
- Wound botulism occurs when wounds are infected with *C. botulinum* that secretes the toxin.

With foodborne botulism, symptoms begin within 6 hours to 10 days (most commonly between 12 and 36 hours) after eating food that contains the toxin. Symptoms of botulism include double vision, blurred vision, drooping eyelids, slurred speech, difficulty swallowing, dry mouth, and muscle weakness that moves down the body, usually affecting the shoulders first, then the upper arms, lower arms, thighs, calves, etc. Paralysis of breathing muscles can cause a person to stop breathing and die, unless assistance with breathing (mechanical ventilation) is provided.

Botulism is not spread from one person to another. Foodborne botulism can occur in all age groups.

A supply of antitoxin against infant botulism is maintained by the California Department of Public Health's Infant Botulism Treatment and Prevention Program, and a supply of antitoxin against other kinds of botulism is maintained by CDC. The antitoxin is most effective in reducing the severity of symptoms if administered early in the course of the disease. Most patients eventually recover after weeks to months of supportive care.

Pathway to an *Addiction Free* Lifestyle

MRSA Infection

(Methicillin-resistant Staphylococcus aureus)

Historical Overview of MRSA

In order to better understand the history and development of methicillin-resistant Staphylococcus aureus (MRSA), we need to start from the development of the antibiotic drug penicillin, which is integral to this topic. Penicillin was introduced in 1941 and it was only one year later, in 1942, that penicillin-resistant strains of Staphylococcus aureus were first reported in hospitalized patients. Community strains of S. aureus remained sensitive to penicillin for several years. By the 1970s, penicillin resistance was widespread in the community as well as within healthcare facilities.

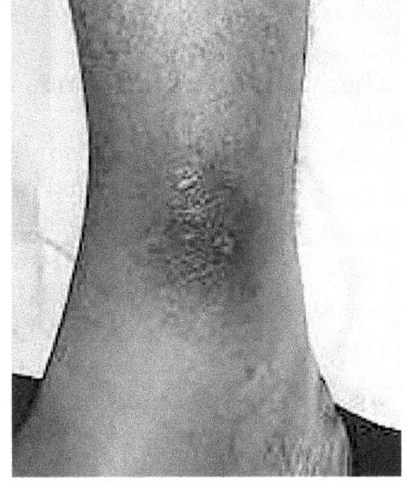

Methicillin, a semi-synthetic penicillin derivative, was introduced in 1960. MRSA had been identified within a short period of time after methicillin was first applied to the handling of Staphylococcus aureus and other types of infectious bacteria. The first nosocomial (hospital) outbreak in the United States occurred in 1968 in Boston, Massachusetts. MRSA made its first major public appearance in the United States in 1981 among intravenous drug users. Staphylococcus aureus is often called a "superbug" because of its power to adapt and become immune to many types of antibiotics. Staph infections, including MRSA, occur most frequently among persons who have weakened immune systems in hospitals and other healthcare facilities, such as nursing homes and kidney dialysis centers. These healthcare-associated staph infections can take the form of surgical wound infections, urinary tract infections, bloodstream infections (sepsis) and pneumonia. It is easy to learn and recognize most of the symptoms of MRSA, which are described in detail on the symptoms page.

MRSA Categorization by Source of Infection

In the scientific literature, MRSA infections are categorized into three groups by where the Staphylococcus aureus bacteria are acquired:

HA-MRSA refers to hospital or healthcare-acquired methicillin-resistant Staphylococcus aureus. Nosocomial infections are acquired in a hospital or other healthcare related institution or in individuals receiving healthcare, such as kidney dialysis, on an ongoing basis. According to the U.S. Centers for Disease Control and Prevention (CDC), the govermental body responsible for tracking infectious diseases, more than 85% of MRSA infections take place in healthcare facilities, making MRSA one of the most common nosocomial infection risks.

CA-MRSA is also known as community-acquired MRSA. This type of MRSA occurs in individuals in the community who are generally healthy and not receiving healthcare in a hospital or on an ongoing outpatient basis. In the last few years, there have been more and more outbreaks of this type reported in communities, meaning that MRSA infections are spreading out of hospitals and healthcare facilities and infecting the general public. Community health professionals are urging people to be more aware of MRSA as a growing threat.

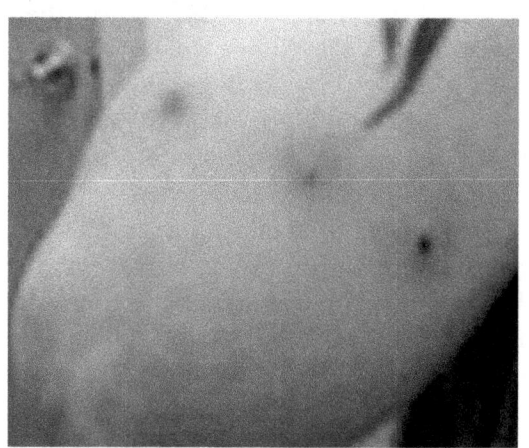

EMRSA is also known as epidemic-type MRSA. A MRSA epidemic is defined differently in different countries. In the United Kingdom, for example, a MRSA epidemic occurs when two or more MRSA isolates are reported in two or more different medical facilities. In the United States, a MRSA outbreak is defined as either three or more nosocomially-acquired MRSA cases that are linked by some epidemiologic variable, or a drastic increase in the number of MRSA cases in a healthcare facility with endemic MRSA. A MRSA outbreak may be defined differently in different healthcare facilities.

Basic Features and Description

The most common type of MRSA infection is a skin infection, but this infection can affect other parts of the body or spread. In severe cases, MRSA infections may cause death due to septic shock or other complications of infection. Diagnosis of MRSA and testing for MRSA infections are described on the MRSA Diagnosis and Testing page in greater detail.

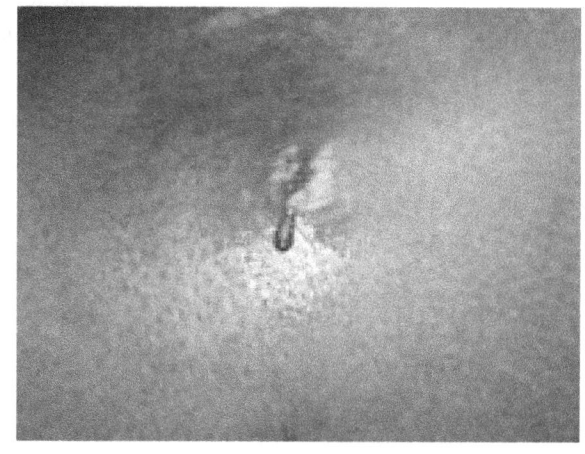

Methicillin-resistant Staphylococcus aureus infections may progress substantially within a day or two of the appearance of the first topical symptoms. MRSA infections are less likely to respond to treatment as the infection progresses. Usually, the initial symptom of the MRSA skin infection is small red bumps on the skin that may resemble pimples or spider bites, with or without fever. Within a couple of days, the bumps on the skin may get larger and become painful, eventually opening into deep, pus-filled boils.

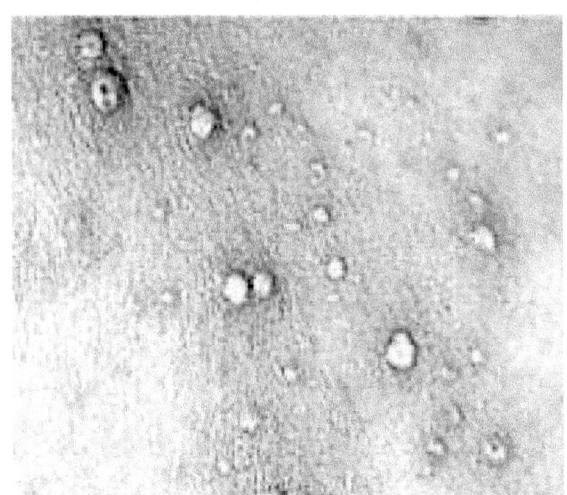

If the infection has not spread too much, the MRSA infection can usually be successfully treated with antibiotic drugs. MRSA infections are defined by their resistance to the once-effective antibiotic drug methicillin. Over time, however, some strains of MRSA have evolved to become immune to other antibiotic drugs as well. This type of infection is called a multi-drug-resistant Staphylococcus aureus infection. Some strains of staph may be resistant to penicillin, methicillin, amoxicillin, oxacillin and some other antibiotics. While there is usually an antibiotic drug that can be used to destroy the bacteria causing the infection, Staphylococcus aureus is particularly good at adapting to new antibiotics. For more information about treatment of MRSA infections, see the MRSA Treatment page.

MRSA can cause serious problems when it spreads to other parts of the body. If MRSA infections involve internal organs, a patient may experience life-threatening complications. Regardless of whether a MRSA infection was acquired nosocomially or in the community, if the infection is not treated it can cause severe complications, such as: endocarditis, septic shock, osteomyelitis, necrotizing fasciitis and even death.

Resources:
Centers for Disease Control and Prevention (CDC)
PubMed Health

Pathway to an *Addiction Free* Lifestyle

Prevention of Recurrent MRSA Skin Infections: What You Need To Know

Clinicians often prescribe topical, intranasal, or systemic antimicrobial agents to patients with recurrent skin infections caused by methicillin-resistant Staphylococcus aureus (MRSA) in an effort to eradicate the staphylococcal carrier state. Some agents can temporarily interrupt staphylococcal carriage, but none has been proved effective for prevention of skin infections caused by MRSA. Extant data do not support the routine prescription of topical antiseptics or of intranasal or systemic antibiotics for the prevention of MRSA skin infections. Hygienic interventions, especially frequent hand washing with plain soap and the use of alcohol-based hand sanitizers, remain the cornerstone of efforts to prevent recurrent infections.

Methicillin-resistant *Staphylococcus aureus* (MRSA) was once considered a strictly nosocomial pathogen. Over the past decade, however, MRSA has emerged as a prominent cause of community-associated infections in both adults and children. Although community-associated MRSA strains occasionally cause severe invasive infections, they are most frequently isolated from patients with skin and soft tissue infections. Furunculosis ("boils") is the most frequently reported manifestation of communityassociated MRSA skin infection, but impetigo, pustulosis, cellulitis, and locally invasive abscesses have also been described.

The tendency of staphylococcal skin infections to recur is well recognized. Data on the frequency of recurrence, however, are sparse. In a study of 69 children who were treated for MRSA skin or soft tissue abscesses, 12% had a history of previous cutaneous abscesses.3 Other studies, which principally involved men with HIV infection, documented recurrences of MRSA skin infections in 31% to 45% of subjects.

In the absence of an effective *S aureus* vaccine, many clinicians recommend various topical, intranasal, or systemic antimicrobial agents for patients with recurrent MRSA skin infections in an effort to "decolonize" them of MRSA. However, there is scant evidence that decolonization strategies actually prevent recurrent MRSA skin infections. In this article, I discuss some of the most popular decolonization strategies and review the evidence regarding their safety and effectiveness.

MRSA infections facts

- MRSA means methicillin-resistant *Staphylococcus aureus* bacteria.

- The majority of MRSA infections are classified as CA-MRSA (community acquired) or HA-MRSA (hospital- or health-care-acquired).

- MRSA infections are transmitted from person to person by direct contact with the skin, clothing, or area (for example, sink, bench, bed, and utensil) that had recent physical contact with a MRSA-infected person.

- The majority of CA-MRSA starts as skin infections; HA-MRSA can begin an infection of the skin, a wound (often a surgical site), or a location where medical devices are placed (catheters, IV lines, or other devices).

- Cellulitis, abscess, or draining pus is often one of the first signs and symptoms of MRSA infections.

- Most MRSA infections are diagnosed by culture and antibiotic sensitivity testing of *Staphylococcus aureus* bacteria isolated from an infected site; a PCR test is also available.

- Currently, MRSA bacteria are almost always found to be resistant to multiple antibiotics. All isolated MRSA strains need to have antibiotic susceptibility determined to choose the correct or appropriate antibiotic therapy.

- Treatment of HA-MRSA frequently involves the use of vancomycin, often in combination with other antibiotics given by IV; CA-MRSA can often be treated on an outpatient basis with specific oral or topical antibiotics, but some serious CA-MRSA infections (for example, pneumonia) often require appropriate antibiotics by IV.

- Prevention of MRSA is possible by excellent hygiene practices, avoiding skin contact with infected people or items they have touched, and by wearing disposable gloves, gowns, and masks when treating or visiting hospitalized MRSA patients. Covering skin abrasions and minor lacerations immediately may also help prevent MRSA infections, especially in children and in people involved in group sports activities.

- **What is methicillin-resistant *Staphylococcus aureus* (MRSA)?**

- MRSA stands for methicillin-resistant *Staphylococcus aureus* (*S. aureus*) bacteria. This organism is known for causing skin infections in addition to many other types of infections. There are other designations in the scientific literature for these bacteria according to where the bacteria are acquired by patients, such as community-acquired MRSA (also termed CA-MRSA or CMRSA), hospital-acquired or health-care-acquired MRSA (also termed HA-MRSA or HMRSA), or epidemic MRSA (EMRSA). Statistical data suggest that as many as 19,000 people per year have died from MRSA in the U.S.; data supplied by the CDC in 2010 suggest this number has declined by about 28% from 2005 to 2008, in part, because of prevention practices at hospitals and home care.

- Although *S. aureus* has been causing infections (Staph infections) probably as long as the human race has existed, MRSA has a relatively short history. MRSA was first noted in 1961, about two years after the antibiotic methicillin was initially used to treat *S. aureus* and other infectious bacteria. The resistance to methicillin was due to a penicillin-binding protein coded for by a mobile genetic element termed the methicillin-resistant gene (mecA). In recent years, the gene has continued to evolve so that many MRSA strains are currently resistant to several different antibiotics such as penicillin, oxacillin, and amoxicillin (Amoxil, Dispermox, Trimox). HA-MRSA are often also resistant to tetracycline (Sumycin), erythromycin (E-Mycin, Eryc, Ery-Tab, PCE, Pediazole, Ilosone), and clindamycin (Cleocin). In 2009, research showed that many antibiotic-resistant genes and toxins are bundled and transferred together to other bacteria, which speed the development of toxic and resistant strains of MRSA. *S. aureus* is sometimes termed a "superbug" because of its ability to be resistant to several antibiotics.

Pathway to an *Addiction Free* Lifestyle

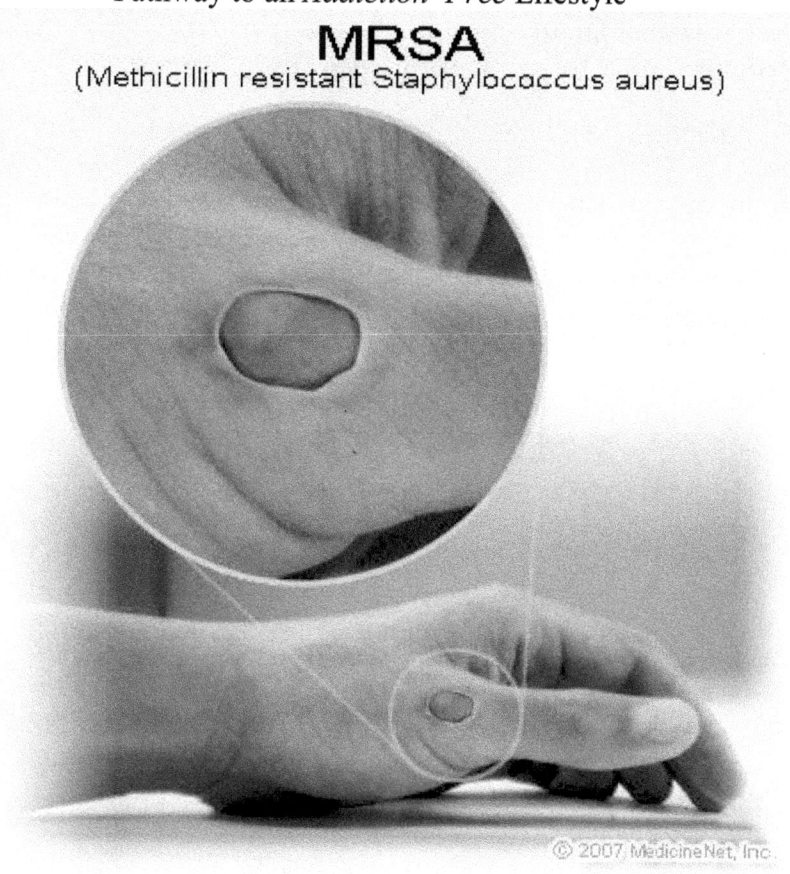

- What does a MRSA infection look like?

- In addition, these organisms have been termed "flesh-eating bacteria" because of their occasional rapid spread and destruction of human skin. Additionally, a number of older (2004-2008) web and popular press articles are titled or include the erroneous term "MRSA virus." This is a misnomer that has confused many people; there is no contagious MRSA virus, and if readers examine these articles, they may realize the content is usually about MRSA bacteria.

- Unfortunately, MRSA strains of bacteria can be found worldwide. In general, healthy people with no cuts, abrasions, or breaks on their skin are at low risk for getting infected. However, the bacteria can be passed from person to person by direct contact with infected skin, mucus, or droplets spread by coughs in both adults and children. Indirect contact also can spread the bacteria; for example, touching items like towels, utensils, clothing, or other objects that have been in contact with an infected person can spread the bacteria to other uninfected individuals. Investigators estimate that about one out of every 100 people in the U.S. are colonized with MRSA (have the organisms in or on their body but not causing infection), and these individuals may transmit MRSA bacteria to others by the same methods listed above. Another term for people colonized with MRSA is "carrier" which means the person carries the organism in or on the body and may transfer the organism to another person who subsequently may become infected. A common place for carriers to harbor MRSA organisms is the nose.

What does a MRSA infection look like?

On the skin, MRSA infection may begin as a reddish rash with lesion(s) that looks like a pimple or small boil. Often it progresses to an open, inflamed area of skin (as pictured below) that may weep pus or drain other similar fluid. In some instances, it may appear as an abscess, a swollen, tender area, often with reddish skin covering. When the abscess is cut open or spontaneously bursts open, pus drains from the area (see Figure 2). See the first web citation for more clinical MRSA pictures, or see the MRSA slideshow listed above.

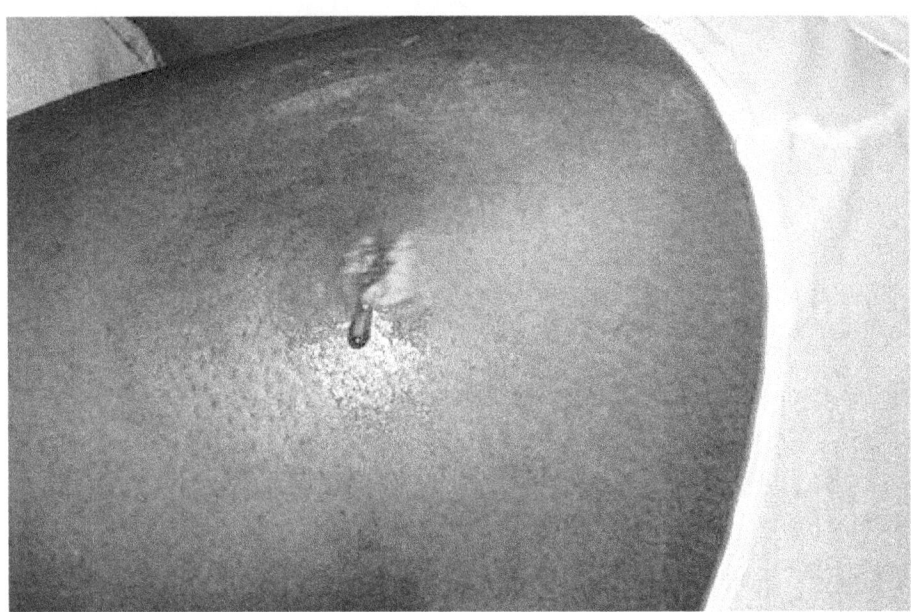

Figure 2: Picture of a MRSA abscess. SOURCE: CDC/Bruno Coignard, MD; Jeff Hageman, MHS

What are the signs and symptoms of MRSA infection?

Most MRSA infections are skin infections that produce the following signs and symptoms:

- Cellulitis (infection of the skin or the fat and tissues that lie immediately beneath the skin, usually starting as small red bumps in the skin with some areas resembling a bruise)

- Boils (pus-filled infections of hair follicles)

- Abscesses (collections of pus in or under the skin; see Fig. 2)

- Sty (an infection of an oil gland of the eyelid)

- Carbuncles (infections larger than an abscess, usually with several openings to the skin)

- Impetigo (a skin infection with pus-filled blisters)

- Rash (skin appears to be reddish or have red-colored areas)

Most of the above signs and symptoms represent the early stages of MRSA infections. One major problem with MRSA (and occasionally with other Staph infections) is that occasionally the skin infection can spread to almost any other organ in the body. When this happens, more severe symptoms develop. MRSA that spreads to internal organs can become life threatening. Fever, chills, low blood pressure, joint pains, severe headaches, shortness of breath, and "rash over most of the body" are symptoms that need immediate medical attention, especially when associated with skin infections. Some CA-MRSA and HA-MRSA infections become severe, and complications such as endocarditis, necrotizing fasciitis, osteomyelitis, sepsis, and death may occur.

How is MRSA infection transmitted or spread?

MRSA infections can be contagious from person to person; occasionally direct contact with a MRSA-infected person is not necessary because the bacteria can also be spread by people who touch materials or surfaces contaminated with MRSA organisms. There are two major ways people become infected with MRSA. The first is physical contact with someone who is either infected or is a carrier (people who are not infected but are colonized with the bacteria on their body) of MRSA. The second way is for people to physically contact MRSA on any objects such as door handles, floors, sinks, or towels that have been touched by a MRSA-infected person or carrier. Normal skin tissue in people usually does not allow MRSA infection to develop; however, if there are cuts, abrasions, or other skin flaws such as psoriasis (a chronic inflammatory skin disease with dry patches, redness, and scaly skin), MRSA may proliferate. Many otherwise healthy individuals, especially children and young adults, do not notice small skin imperfections or scrapes and may be lax in taking precautions about skin contacts. This is the likely reason MRSA outbreaks occur in diverse types of people such as school team players (like football players or wrestlers), dormitory residents, and armed-services personnel in constant close contact.

People with higher risk of MRSA infection are those with obvious skin breaks (for example, patients with surgical or traumatic wounds or hospital patients with intravenous lines, burns, or skin ulcers) and people with depressed immune systems (infants, the elderly, or HIV-infected individuals) or those with chronic diseases (diabetes or cancer). People with pneumonia (lung infection) due to MRSA can transmit MRSA by airborne droplets. Health-care workers as a group are repeatedly exposed to MRSA-positive patients and can have a high rate of infection if precautions are not taken. Consequently, health-care workers and patient visitors should use disposable masks, gowns, and gloves when they enter the MRSA-infected patient's room. As long as people, including carriers, have MRSA organisms in wounds or droplets that are shed into the environment, they are contagious. Carriers must be very careful about personal hygiene (especially coughs, itching or scratching skin, and sneezing) as they may be contagious indefinitely.

How is MRSA diagnosed?

Most doctors start with a complete history and physical exam of the patient to identify any skin changes that may be due to MRSA, especially if the patient or caretaker mentions a close association with a person who has been diagnosed with MRSA. A skin sample, sample of pus from a wound, or blood, urine, or biopsy material (tissue sample) is sent to a microbiology lab and cultured for *S. aureus*. If *S. aureus* is isolated (grown on a Petri plate), the bacteria are then exposed to different antibiotics, including methicillin. *S. aureus* bacteria that grow well when methicillin is in the culture are termed MRSA, and the patient is diagnosed as MRSA infected. The same procedure is done to determine if someone is a MRSA carrier (screening for a carrier), but sample skin or mucous membrane sites are only swabbed, not biopsied. These tests help distinguish MRSA infections from other skin changes that often appear initially similar to MRSA, such as spider bites and skin changes that occur with Lyme disease. These tests are very important; misidentification of a MRSA infection may cause the patient to be treated with other agents like dapsone (used for spider bites). This can result in progression of the MRSA infection and even other complications due to the dapsone.

In 2008, the U.S. Food and Drug Administration (FDA) approved a rapid blood test (StaphSR assay) that can detect the presence of MRSA genetic material in a blood sample in as little as two hours. The test is also able to determine whether the genetic material is from MRSA or from less dangerous forms of Staph bacteria. The test (PCR based) is not recommended for use in monitoring treatment of MRSA infections and should not be used as the only basis for the diagnosis of a MRSA infection. In addition, there are new screening tests that report detecting or ruling out MRSA infections in about five hours.

How can people prevent MRSA infection?

Not making direct contact with skin, clothing, and any items that come in contact with either MRSA patients or MRSA carriers is the best way to avoid MRSA infection. In many instances, this situation is simply not practical because such infected individuals or carriers are not immediately identifiable. What people can do is to treat and cover (for example, antiseptic cream and a Band-Aid) any skin breaks or wounds and use excellent hygiene practices (for example, hand washing with soap after personal contact or toilet use, washing clothes that potentially came in contact with MRSA patients or carriers, and using disposable items when treating MRSA patients). Also available at most stores are antiseptic solutions and wipes to both clean hands and surfaces that may contact MRSA. These measures help control the spread of MRSA.

Pregnant women need to consult with their doctors if they are infected with or are carriers of MRSA. Although MRSA is not transmitted to infants by breastfeeding, there are a few reports that infants can be infected by their mothers who have MRSA, but this seems to be an infrequent situation. Some pregnant MRSA carriers have been successfully treated with the antibiotic mupirocin cream (Bactroban).

In 2007, the first incidence of MRSA in a pet was recorded. Although relatively rare, MRSA can be transferred between pets and humans. MRSA has been documented in dogs, cats, and horses but may be found in other animals in the future. Care and treatments are similar to those in humans, but a veterinarian should be consulted on all potential cases.

MRSA has been isolated from the environment (for example, beach sand and water), but there is no good documentation that people have become infected from these sources. Most authors suggest prevention methods should consist of a good soap and water shower after visiting the beach.

The CDC does not recommend (2010 guidelines) general screening of patients for MRSA. However, the CDC does recommend that high-risk patients who are being admitted to the hospital be screened for MRSA and then, if positive for MRSA, follow infection-control guidelines during the hospital stay. A recent study showed that the number of infections with both HA-MRSA and CA-MRSA has dropped since 2005-2008, and authorities speculate that such drops are due to infection-control measures in hospitals and better home-care measures (listed below).

How should caregivers treat MRSA patients at home?

The CDC states (2010 guidelines) that healthy caregivers are unlikely to become infected while caring for MRSA patients at home if they do the following:

- Caregivers should wash their hands with soap and water after physical contact with the infected or colonized person and before leaving the home.

- Towels used for drying hands after contact should be used only once.

- Disposable gloves should be worn if contact with body fluids is expected, and hands should be washed after removing the gloves.

- Linens should be changed and washed on a routine basis, especially if they are soiled.

- The patient's environment should be cleaned routinely and when soiled with body fluids.

- Notify doctors and other health-care personnel who provide care for the patient that the patient is colonized or infected with a multidrug-resistant organism.

What is the prognosis (outlook), and what are the potential complications for people with MRSA infections?

Statistics from the Kaiser foundation in 2007 (http://www.kaisernetwork.org/daily_reports/rep_index.cfm?DR_ID=45809) indicated that about 1.2 million hospitalized patients have MRSA, and the mortality (death) rate was estimated to be between 4%-10%. These data have not been updated by the CDC yet. Another study suggested that the mortality rate may be as high as 23%. In general, the average adult death rate was about 5% of infected patients in 2010. Fortunately, in children under 18 years of age, a recent (2009) study suggests their mortality rate is much lower (about 1%), even though the number of hospitalized children with MRSA has almost tripled since 2002. In general, CA-MRSA has far less risk of any complications than HA-MRSA as long as the patient does well with treatment and does not require hospitalization. However, people who do suffer complications generally have a chance for a worse outcome, as organ systems may be irreversibly damaged. Complications from MRSA can occur in almost all organ systems; the following is a listing of some that can result in permanent organ damage or death: endocarditis, kidney or lung infections (pneumonia), necrotizing fasciitis, osteomyelitis, and sepsis. Early diagnosis and treatment usually result in better outcomes and reduction or elimination of further complications.

What is the treatment for MRSA infection?

Pathway to an *Addiction Free* Lifestyle

As stated by the U.S. Centers for Disease Control and Prevention (CDC):

- "First-line treatment for mild abscesses is incision and drainage."

- "If antibiotic treatment is clinically indicated, it should be guided by the susceptibility profile of the organism." When the tests are run to determine that the Staph bacteria isolated from a given patient are methicillin resistant, these tests also provide information about which antibiotics can successfully kill the bacteria (its susceptibility profile)."

Fortunately, many MRSA infections still can be treated by certain specific antibiotics (for example, vancomycin [Vancocin], linezolid [Zyvox], and others, often in combination with vancomycin). Most moderate to severe infections need to be treated by intravenous antibiotics, usually given in the hospital setting. Some CA-MRSA strains are susceptible to trimethoprim-sulfamethoxazole (Bactrim), doxycycline (Vibramycin), and clindamycin (Cleocin); although reports suggest clindamycin resistance is increasing rapidly. In addition, some strains are now resistant to vancomycin. In 2011, researchers developed a chemical change in the antibiotic vancomycin that rendered vancomycin-resistant MRSA susceptible to the drug. It is not available commercially, but this discovery, along with ongoing research, is important because it may expand treatment possibilities for MRSA and other drug-resistant bacteria such as VRE (vancomycin-resistant enterococci).

A good medical practice is to determine, by microbiological techniques done in a lab, which antibiotic(s) can kill the MRSA and use it alone or, more often, in combination with additional antibiotics to treat the infected patient. Since resistance can change quickly, antibiotic treatments may need to change also. Many people think they are "cured" after a few antibiotic doses and stop taking the medicine. This is a bad decision because the MRSA may still be viable in or on the person and thus is capable of reinfecting the person or others. Also, the surviving MRSA may be exposed to low antibiotic doses when the medicine is stopped too soon; this low dose may allow MRSA enough time to become resistant to the medicine. Consequently, MRSA patients (in fact, all patients) treated with appropriate antibiotics should take the entire course of the antibiotic as directed by their doctor. A note of caution is that, in the last few years, there have been reports of a new strain of MRSA that is resistant to vancomycin (VRSA or vancomycin-resistant *S. aureus*) and other antibiotics. Currently, VRSA is detected more often than a few years ago, but if it becomes widespread, it may be the next "superbug."

What is a "superbug"?

The term "superbug" is a nonspecific word that is used to describe any microorganism that is resistant to at least one or more commonly used antibiotics. Some authors restrict its use to microorganisms resistant to two or more antibiotics. Unfortunately, the term *superbug* is used in the medical and popular press to describe several different types of organisms which can lead readers to be confused about specific diseases and the infectious agents that cause them. The most common bacteria described as superbugs are the following:

- MRSA (*Staphylococcus aureus* strains resistant to multiple antibiotics)

- VRE (*Enterococcus* species resistant to vancomycin)

- PRSP (*Streptococcus pneumoniae* strains resistant to penicillin)

- ESBLs (*Escherichia coli* and other Gram-negative bacteria resistant to antibiotics such as cephalosporins and monobactams)

Emerging superbugs may include multiple drug-resistant *Clostridium difficile*, VRSA (vancomycin-resistant *S. aureus*), and NDM *Escherichia coli* (New Delhi metallo-beta-lactamase resistant *E. coli*).

Where are other MRSA information sources?

http://www.emedicinehealth.com/slideshow_mrsa_pictures/article_em.htm

http://www.cdc.gov/mrsa/index.html

http://www.pnas.org/cgi/content/full/99/11/7687

http://www.cdc.gov/ncidod/EID/vol11no06/04-0831.htm

http://www.kaisernetwork.org/daily_reports/rep_index.cfm?DR_ID=45809

http://www.cdc.gov/ncidod/dhqp/ar_multidrugFAQ.html

http://pubs.acs.org/doi/abs/10.1021/ja207142h

REFERENCES:

eMedicine.com. *Staphylococcus aureus* Infections, 2009.

Pathway to an *Addiction Free* Lifestyle

www.ingramcontent.com/pod-product-compliance
Lightning Source LLC
Chambersburg PA
CBHW080529170426
43195CB00016B/2511